Praise for

Hey, Jesus, It's Me

"Ellen Skrmetti is a national treasure, tackling some of life's most perplexing moments with the infectious humor and sassy elegance that only a true Southern queen can! Her faith is infused throughout this book full of heartfelt, hilarious stories that will feel familiar no matter where you call home. Ellen is a gift of pure joy, especially for a 'cups and ice' chick like me!"

—Shannon Bream, #1 *New York Times* bestselling author and anchor of *Fox News Sunday*

"Angels who make us laugh are a gift from above. Ellen is part sweet and part salty with a lot of Southern funny mixed in. A daily dose of her humor is good for my soul."

—Roma Downey, actress, producer, and *New York Times* bestselling author

"Ellen has a sharp wit and a soft heart that will keep you turning the page. Her book is perfect for anyone that needs to keep Jesus on speed dial."

—Laura Rutledge, host and reporter for ESPN and the SEC Network

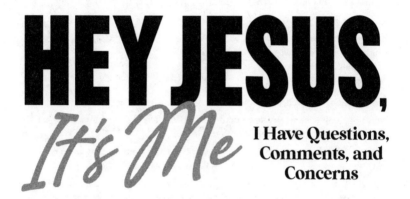

HEY JESUS, It's Me

I Have Questions, Comments, and Concerns

Ellen Skrmetti

New York · Nashville

Worthy
Hachette Book Group
1290 Avenue of the Americas, New York, NY 10104
worthypublishing.com
twitter.com/worthypub

First Edition: September 2024

Worthy is a division of Hachette Book Group, Inc. The Worthy name and logo are registered trademarks of Hachette Book Group, Inc.

The publisher is not responsible for websites (or their content) that are not owned by the publisher.

The Hachette Speakers Bureau provides a wide range of authors for speaking events. To find out more, go to hachettespeakersbureau.com or email HachetteSpeakers@hbgusa.com.

Worthy Books may be purchased in bulk for business, educational, or promotional use. For information, please contact your local bookseller or the Hachette Book Group Special Markets Department at special.markets@hbgusa.com.

Library of Congress Cataloging-in-Publication Data
Names: Skrmetti, Ellen, author.
Title: Hey, Jesus, it's me : I have questions, comments, and concerns / Ellen
   Skrmetti.
Description: New York, NY : Worthy, [2024]
Identifiers: LCCN 2024002832 | ISBN 9781546007043 (hardcover) | ISBN
   9781546007074 (ebook)
Subjects: LCSH: Christianity—Humor. | Prayer—Humor. | American wit and
   humor. | LCGFT: Humor. | Essays.
Classification: LCC PN6231.C35 S56 2024 | DDC 230.002/07—dc23/eng/20240409
LC record available at https://lccn.loc.gov/2024002832

ISBNs: 978-1-5460-0704-3 (hardcover); 978-1-5460-0707-4 (ebook)

Printed in the United States of America

LSC-C

Printing 1, 2024

For Tim, Meg, and Nik.
I love you anything you say plus one.

Contents

Contents

Introduction

RUN INTO A FELLOW SOUTHERN woman and the conversation will somehow find its way to mamas, menus, or menopause. We'll talk about unspoken prayer requests and compare notes, but we are NOT being nosy. We're trying to do the Lord's work by helping him answer infinite prayers as efficiently as possible.

Call it a church thing, a Southern thing, or a woman thing, but we share certain stories and experiences that make us all want to rake up kin. We've all had our mama tell us to act natural when Great Aunt Flora takes her teeth out after she eats. And we've all been told to say our *yes, ma'am*s and *no, ma'am*s and to keep our freezers ready in case someone up and dies.

This book is for you if:

- you've ever said, "Let me put that bug in your ear";
- you've heard "Who made the dressin'?" but it wasn't a compliment;

- you have ever sat in Sunday service and thought, *Surely some of these people won't make it to the sweet by-and-by with me*;
- your skills for uncovering the subject behind an "unspoken prayer request" could be used by the FBI to solve crimes;
- you run fans in the dead of winter;
- you brought a casserole to the church social and have been on cups and ice ever since;
- your granny died on a Monday and was in the ground by Wednesday; or
- you have NEVER said or heard any of these things but are intrigued.

I named this book *Hey, Jesus, It's Me* after my most popular Web series. I started my "Hey, Jesus" calls in hopes that it would remind people that Jesus wants our laughter along with our tears. He is truly a loving God and wants to be part of every moment of our lives—even our silly questions, comments, and concerns. Though I have been asked many times for the number I'm calling and if I can lend out my remote,* I love that I don't

---

* The prop I use in my videos. I film on my phone, so I need something that I can use that looks like a phone.

need to. We all have a direct line already. At any time, we can say, "Hey, Jesus, it's me," and he's right there—no need to give the last four digits of your social, your mama's maiden name, or the street you grew up on... He's always right there.

Instagram likes sketches that are short and sweet, but I'm more long-winded and salty, and these stories give more insight into my life, my raisin', and the meaning behind some of my most popular sketches. My prayer is that these stories make you laugh a lot, cry a little, and inspire you to talk to Jesus even more.

CAUGHT BETWEEN A ROCK AND A HOT FLASH

JUST THINKING OF PERIMENOPAUSE sends a hot flash down my spine. There was a time I thought I was going to escape the perils of menopause, but now that I've come face-to-face with things like travel fans, cooling sheets, and cooling pajamas, I know that not only am I not going to escape, but I'm headed straight for it.

When I started my menopause journey, I gave my mother a huge apology because our family of jokesters did not make her menopause years easy on her. Once, we were driving to Memphis and she said that she needed to buy a drink at our next stop because she had forgotten to take her hormones and nerve pills.* As soon as she said it, my brother and I started yelling, "Dad! Pull over, pull over! Mama needs her pills!" and Dad made it worse by doing a dramatic speedup to get to the next gas station.

We did help Mom with the hot flashes by keeping our house like an igloo. I'm not sure how low the temperature was, but each time my feet get cold, I'm reminded of home. Not everyone was as accustomed to the freezing temps in our house. I can still see my brother's girlfriend, who is now my sister-in-love, Shannon, coming over to our house with her very own blanket in tow. "Everybody put your coats on. Mama's having a hot flash, so we have to turn on the air-conditionin' on Christmas Eve."

Oh, how the tables have turned. Mom's hormone pills have been replaced with blood thinners, and I'm now the one longing to live in cold storage. Even worse, when I go home to visit, Mom has the air either turned

---

* A good Southern woman would never give the name of her actual medicine. *Nerve pill* gives plenty of explanation.

off or set to seventy-six. Last year I was helping cook dinner and I asked my mom if we could please open the door because I was burning up.

"Ellen, it's below thirty out there," my mom said.

"Ok. I'll just step outside for five minutes and come back inside to thaw out," I said.

When I apologized to my mom for the hard time we gave her while she was going through the change, she said, "Well, I gave you a lot of comedic material while I was going through it."

"Speaking of," I asked her, "that time you threw the tree out the back door—was that menopause related?"

Each year we bought a live Christmas tree and Mama loaded that tree with lights and ornaments until it begged for mercy. One year, we picked a tree that was NOT up for the job, and it fell over twice. Each time, Mom picked up the tree, and she, my dad, and my brother helped tighten it back into its stand while I helped clean up needles and put the ornaments back on. But when that poor tree fell a third time, Mama had had enough. With the strength that can only come from a frustrated mama, she picked up the tree all by herself, walked it from the dining room to the den, and threw it out the back door. It had taken three people to get it in the house, and ONE MAD MAMA to get it out!

"No! The tree incident wasn't menopause, and before you start, it's not because I'm crazy. It's because I'm colorful."

And the world needs colorful women.

1

MEN GET HOT, WOMEN SWEAT

Hey, Jesus, it's me. Listen, can you please help me understand why my husband is over here getting hotter with age, while I'm just...hot. And I don't mean just hot. He's getting cuter by the minute, and I'm over here melting.

I DON'T THINK I'LL EVER FORGET MY first hot flash. The heat started deeper in my soul than I thought possible and came right up to my neck.

Why is this on my neck? Why is this called a hot flash? Flashes are short. This isn't short! A man must've named this.

As I lay burning, I looked over at my husband in peaceful slumber, not a care in the world. His hair had gracefully gone gray—he's what some would call a silver fox.

Oh my word, if I sweat any more in this bed, I'm going to have to change the sheets.

His vision had gotten so weak he could no longer see in any light other than bright sunlight, but he'd started wearing readers, which only made him hotter. He offered them to me once, and I absolutely DO need them since I can't see a thing up close, but I refused to wear them. I have enough problems without looking like Grandma Moses.

My personal little summer finally ended, and I tried

to pull myself back together. I wanted to get back to sleep, but my brain was working harder than a rented mule. Was this it? Was this the end of the line? I didn't feel like I was dying, but I did feel like my best years were behind me. And who could blame me?

When I got my eyebrows waxed, I'd had to get my lip done too, then my chin. Why am I getting hair on my chin anyway?

Forget dieting.

The mere thought of a donut made my clothes tight.

I was nearing the top of the Zippin Pippin, and I was about to go downhill full steam ahead.*

Before I could fill my closet with those polyester suit sets that the old ladies used to wear to church, I heard a voice whisper,

You're not done yet.

I recognized it. I'd heard this voice before.

Oh, I think we're done, at least with comedy. I'm what, forty-four, forty-five, and it still hasn't happened.

---

* The Zippin Pippin is one of the oldest wooden roller coasters in the United States and was at the Mid-South Fair and Libertyland in Memphis forever.

If it were meant to be, I would have been discovered by now.

And then the voice said,

That is literally the stupidest thing I have ever heard.

This was the same voice that said, *I never took that bet* when I claimed stage fright was the reason I never stepped onstage after Miss Mississippi. I was about to take the stage for the talent competition when stage fright filled my body for the first time ever. Before I went onstage, I prayed, *Lord, if you will get me off this stage, then I will never get on another stage again.*

The problem wasn't that I prayed the prayer—the problem was that I thought it was true and that the Lord would make a deal with a scared eighteen-year-old and hold her to it. Now I know—God is a waymaker, not a dealmaker.

Years later, once I realized that my stage fright was most likely the devil using my fear to keep me from living my dream, I got busy.

I found a local comedy club that offered stand-up classes one night a week. I spent months learning to write jokes before I finally got onstage. It was only five minutes, but my fear was conquered.

That was March. March of 2020. The COVID-19 pandemic had begun, and the next day Alabama announced that we'd be joining the rest of the world and shutting down for two little ole weeks.

Places that hosted comedy nights offered free toilet paper if you ordered their bar food curbside. Stand-up was down for the count. But I found a ray of hope—major comedy schools that only hosted in-person classes were switching to online formats. I signed up for a class from the Second City...then I took another...then another!

Eventually, businesses began to reopen, but not all of them. The comedy club where I first got onstage was now a doctor's office. Around town, the few open mics that were open started at 11 p.m., but I like to be bra-less by 9. I kept going and studied the great comics. I found a precise formula for "making it":

1. Work in smoky clubs.
2. Get booed off stage.
3. Repeat until you stop getting booed off stage.

That was my plan, and I was going to work it.

Hey, Jesus, it's me. Can you please get me on the stage?

I realized that nobody was going to discover me, because they weren't looking for comedians in the carpool line or at PTO meetings. The fact of the matter was I wasn't going to be discovered the way most comedians were discovered.

I had been praying for God to give me exactly what I wanted, and not what he wanted for me. It dawned on me that I had been praying for him to make MY dreams come true, not for his plans for me to come to fruition. I'd been putting God in a box.

I decided if I was going to be discovered, then I was going to have to throw up my own jazz hands.* There's only one deep ocean where you can find perimenopausal wannabe comedians: the Internet.

I asked my husband, Tim, "Are you ok if I start doing sketches on Instagram?"

I expected him to hesitate or at least ask questions, but he said, "Whatever you need to do is fine with me."

"Um, ok"—trying to talk sense into him—"but you

---

* I call them jazz hands; you may call them spirit fingers. Either way, throw your hands in the air, and let the world know you're here!

don't think you'll be embarrassed having your wife doing stand-up sketches on social media?"

"Nah—everyone knows you're crazy."

I decided to give it a go, but I gave myself a few rules before I started posting sketches:

No trending audio. My goal was to be the visual *and* the audio.

No paying to boost a post. I would build an organic audience one reel at a time.

I would work to be so original that if anyone tried to copy me, it would be obvious.

I wrote some sketches and posted the first one on January 3, 2022. I was praying a different prayer than before. Instead of asking for one specific thing, I tried to think of the boldest prayer I could pray. One that would open up all of the blessings God wanted for me.

So I decided to "go big" and prayed every day and every night,

Lord, please do something so big in my life that it could only be you. Let it be so big that credit can only go to you.

I posted short video sketches five days a week. At

first, my page growth was slow as molasses. When I started feeling like it might be time to hang it up, no more "Hey, Jesus," I remembered a quote from a Joel Osteen book: "You're closer than you think."*

It turned out I *was* closer than I thought. A few weeks after I was thinking of stopping, I posted my sketch "If the Queen Died in the South." It was based on about a million conversations I had heard my mother have with friends and family.

That video went viral, and I kept the content coming.

One thing this experience has taught me is that just because no one is looking for you doesn't mean they won't be happy they found you. Sometimes, people don't know what they're missing until they find it.

Now I think back fondly to the night that I lay burning, when I thought my life was ending just because I'd started menopause, and recognize that it was the beginning of a new chapter. One that I wasn't anticipating, but God knew what he was doing all along.

So, ladies, let the men get silver-haired and sexy!

---

* Joel Osteen, *It's Your Time* (New York: Howard Books, 2009).

We may sweat until we feel fried, but our goose is far from cooked. Our hair color may fade, and the lines may show, but we have stories that only we can tell. Turn your fans on high, throw up your jazz hands even higher, and never stop!

2

MY HEIGHT, MY WEIGHT, MY BUSINESS

Hey, Jesus, it's me. Listen, can you please make sure that my family knows that even if I go missing, there is never a good reason to post my height and weight anywhere? That's right, Jesus. If I'm ever missing to the point that they think, *Maybe if we post her height and weight, we could find her*, then it's already too late. I've passed over. It's time to get your casseroles ready and say goodbye!

I DON'T KNOW WHAT MADE ME STEP ON the scale, but I knew I had to face the music. My weight was getting out of control since we'd moved to Nashville and then to Birmingham a year later. I swear the pointer circled around twice. How does this even happen? A scale has numbers that you think should be impossible for your body to reach, but mine had found a way.

I know the full armor of the Lord is heavy, but this was ridiculous.

I've never been completely honest about my weight. I'm not sure if I was ever taught to lie about my weight, or if it just came naturally to me. All Southern women know these three things: to monogram everything, complain about nothing, and keep your weight to yourself.

Lying about my weight started simply. Girls at school would be mortified when they hit three digits on the scale, but I couldn't remember life in single digits. I think I was born 120 and it grew from there. As they were talking, I would have the same mortified look on my face but for a different reason.

....

Oh, bless your bones—you weigh 103? I'm sure
you'll get it off. Should we pray? Should we
exercise? Should you come a little closer
so I can slap you?

....

My first true white lie was when I got my driver's license. Height: five eight; weight: 125. You *had* to lie. After all, the first thing you do when you get your license is show off your picture. Everyone was going to see it! Plus, it wasn't that big of a lie...I could buy a ThighMaster, get a stomach virus, or eat a tapeworm and get there.

No matter, that number was my number over the next four years.

When I renewed my license as a confident nineteen-year-old I boldly added five pounds to the number. I did the same at each renewal.

I tested my fate on my last renewal. The nice lady behind the counter said, "And are we changing your weight?" With fake confidence I proclaimed, "No! That weight is correct." She looked me square in the face and said, "And that's your business."

It seems all of our moves to new cities had taken a bigger toll than I was ready to admit.

* * *

After fifteen years of living in Jackson, we realized that most of our friends lived there because their family lived there. We lived there because our family didn't. We love our family, but there is something to be said for living close enough to visit but far enough away that you have to call before you come over. And as much as we loved Jackson, we could feel that it was time to move on.

One day, I was at Brent's Drugs* when I got a text from Tim.

Want to move to Nashville? he asked.

I was mentally at Home Depot buying moving boxes before I remembered to respond.

YES!!!!

Who wouldn't want to live in Nashville?? The food... the music...the city...Did I mention the food? We up and moved, and the first six months felt like we were on vacation! I worked for *Nashville Scene* and *Nfocus*, so I had the inside scoop on all the best places to eat.

I also knew that the best cupcakes came from the Cupcake Collection, Noshville was my deli of choice,

---

* Brent's is anything but a drugstore, unless you consider burgers and shakes as medicine, and your drugstore was a set location for *The Help*.

and I had just discovered millionaire's bacon at Brick-Top's on West End Avenue when my coworker/girlfriend Marissa said, "Psst, act cool, but Scotty McCreery is sitting right behind you."

My eyes got as big as soda bottles.

"Remind me what he sings." Have you ever gotten so excited you forget everything you ever knew? I knew who Scotty McCreery was, but all my good sense left my body when I realized I was rubbing shoulders with a country music star.

Marissa leaned in and started crooning in a sexy, deep baritone about turning the lights down, like Josh Turner in his hit tune that Scotty sang when auditioning on *American Idol*.

She had barely sung "low" when I burst out laughing, so loud you would've thought I was at Josh Turner's live concert. Now I can't hear his voice without thinking about Marissa or millionaire's bacon.

Scotty McCreery was my only brush with fame in Nashville, but I left completely educated about where to find good hot chicken, who had the best breakfast in town, and how every company should implement a "bagel Friday" if they want to keep morale high.

After six months of living in Nashville, "vacation

mode" turned off and reality started setting in. We were realizing that this might be the best city to bust your diet but not where WE were meant to plant our roots.

We now joke that Jackson, Mississippi, was too small, and Nashville, Tennessee, was too big, but Birmingham, Alabama, is just right.

As it turns out, Birmingham is Nashville's little cousin when it comes to food, and I was back on another vacation. I discovered SoHo Social, Heavenly Donuts, and Ashley Mac's.

After a year of living in Birmingham, we knew we wanted to plant roots, so we bought a home and made it permanent. Once we were settled in our house, I had to get my new driver's license, which is when I got the eyebrow about keeping my weight the same. Yes, I had enjoyed eating my way through great food cities, but food also numbed the stress of moving two small children across three states.

So, there I was on the scale, watching the pointer circle go around like the Big Wheel on *The Price Is Right*.

I spent a few months thinking, *I am going to embrace this! There is a body-positive movement happening, and I will be part of it!*

But I felt terrible. I had no energy, no self-esteem, and no pants that buttoned. I avoided every camera and mirror, thinking, *Maybe I can love myself if I just never look at myself.*

One afternoon, Tim found me crying in our bedroom, and I tried to explain that I'd never had to lose so much weight in my life. I didn't know where to start. Through my tears, I said, "I'm trying so hard to be one of those larger women that loves themselves, but I can't."

I'll never forget what Tim said in that moment: "I think you are beautiful, but if you don't think you are beautiful, then we need to figure out how to help you see what I see."

Those were the words I needed to hear. He didn't judge me, and he didn't try to fix me. He just loved me.

Weight now in the back seat, I focused on more energy, so I joined a gym. Not just any gym—I joined Orangetheory Fitness right next to my favorite place to buy honey-barbeque and lemon-pepper wings.

I would walk past the gym, watching people running on treadmills and wondering what it was like to do that workout and not die.

I signed up for a free class, and I had one request for

Jesus: *If I die, please have someone just roll my body to the back dumpster and leave me be. Don't let them make a big fuss, and don't let me make the news. My family already knows that this is how I would want it.*

I did survive the workout, but my *everything* hurt. I was aching, sore, and weak, and when I tried to walk down the stairs, I *fell* directly on those steps. It was a special level of hurt I'd never felt before. My kids heard the noise and came to rescue me. I begged them to please look away. One leg was headed north, the other headed south, and my pride was in the gutter.

Someone suggested that the thing to do was to just keep working out, which sounded like a cruel thing to say. I needed a full-body cast, not more of the same. Still, I went back again and again and began to realize that I wasn't the first person in the world with weight to lose, and I wouldn't be the last. And that good things take time.

As time passed, I started standing taller, my clothes got looser, and the number on the scale mattered less and less. As I gained confidence, I stopped worrying so much about getting my old body back. I could lose all the weight in the world, but if I didn't love myself, it wouldn't matter. Which is good because I also learned that the most fun thing about losing weight in your forties is. that. you. *can't*. I mean, you can ... You just can't do it fast.

So, Jesus, it's me. I've reconsidered. If I go missing, will you let my family know they CAN post my height and weight? As long as they understand that it's most likely a lie.

3

ONNAY'ALL IS LYIN'

Hey, Jesus, it's me. Listen, my mother told me that some women go through menopause and have no symptoms, but I'm not seeing anywhere that that is true. Either the doctors are lying, or my mama is lying. It's her? She's lying? Every woman has a symptom? That figures. Sounds like something she would do.

I T'S NOT THAT MY MOTHER HAD BEEN lying to me so much as she had been protecting me in hopes that I was the one human on earth who didn't have to worry about things. I can hear her say, *Well, what if it never happens to you, and here you worried for nothing?*

She was kind to try to protect me, but I do wish she would have prepared me better for one pivotal part of motherhood. Breastfeeding.

My stance on breastfeeding came from a place of pure peer pressure. Yes, the same *If all your friends jumped off a bridge, would you jump?* peer pressure. And don't ask me if I would jump off a bridge if all my friends jumped off a bridge. I had the most amazing group of girlfriends. If they jumped off a bridge, then it was for a good reason. So, yes, we'd all jump off a bridge!

I couldn't name a single friend that formula-fed her baby. I heard friends at work say they could pump so fast they'd make your head spin. Then they'd hide the milk in the fridge under their desks and get back to work lickety-split.

By the time I was pregnant, all of my girlfriends could tell you the pros and cons of every breast pump on the market, and no less than four gave me their leftover nipple cream. My friends knew every trick in the book when it came to surviving nipple torture. They even helped me purchase the best nipple covers to help my boobs on their milk quest. As committed as I was, I found the one line I would not cross. CABBAGE LEAVES. Yes, one friend told me to bring frozen cabbage leaves to work and put them on my breasts if they started to hurt during the day. The idea of setting up a salad bar on my chest at work was too much.

What helped me truly commit to breastfeeding was knowing that I was giving my baby the best nutrition on earth, that it was God's perfect design, and—the cherry on top—that it burned a TON of calories. And I mean a ton! Some books said three hundred calories; others said five hundred. It didn't matter. I decided to get my pre-baby body back by feeding my baby nature's milk around the clock!

I was so committed that I didn't just buy myself

breastfeeding books, but I bought them for my mother too. Formula was in fashion when I was born, but so was smoking,* so we weren't following that generation's lead. For this baby, we were going to be a breastfeeding dynamic duo.

When I left the hospital with Meg, my milk hadn't come in, but the doctor assured me that it would. "Just pump and your body will figure out that it's time."

I pumped, and after twenty minutes, no milk. The bottle was dry.

It's ok, I told myself. *It's gonna come in.*

Then I tried a few hours later...still dry.

Remain calm...It's going to come.

Then I cranked my super-turbo breast pump on HIGH, and I waited and waited. After thirty minutes, the bottle wasn't just dry...It was so clean it could go back in the cabinet.

I cried.

---

* My brother was born in 1973, and my mom said that doctors would smoke with you to celebrate a pregnancy. By the time she was pregnant with me in 1976–77, research had come out linking smoking to low birth weight, and she stopped smoking. My brother would give her grief, saying, "Imagine what I would have become if you hadn't smoked with me."

And when we took our daughter for her three-day checkup, I cried even more. She was losing weight, my colostrum was gone, and I was starving my baby. There was no choice but to formula-feed her. I gave her a formula bottle and decided to try to pump one more time.

I prayed, *Lord, if you want me to breastfeed this baby, then send the milk.* It reminded me of the scene in *Beaches* where Bette Midler's character bangs on the radiator and yells, "Send the heat up!" except unlike Bette's heat, my milk never came.

I cried.

Why did I dread telling my friends that my milk didn't come in? Probably because I was the only woman on earth whose milk *didn't* come in! In all of my breastfeeding books, there wasn't a single chapter titled "So, Your Milk Didn't Come In and Now You're Starving Your Baby and You Aren't Going to Be Burning Any Extra Calories."

At the next checkup, I asked my doctor why it never came in, and he explained that the act of labor sends a signal to your body to send the milk, and it could be that since I was a scheduled C-section and I never had contractions, my body was just asleep at the wheel.

I told my mom that I must be the only woman in history to not be able to breastfeed her own baby.

"Oh no, honey. I remember my mama having to breast-feed for Aunt Flora because her milk never came in."

What did she just say??

"Yeah, it just never came in, and Mama had plenty to spare."*

"Mom! You mean to tell me that someone that I am biologically related to never had their milk come in, and you never thought to tell me??" I exclaimed.

"Well, I just never wanted to worry you. You were so excited, and what if your milk came in and you had worried for nothing?"

"I would have been prepared that this could be something that might happen," I told her.

"Well, it was either going to come in or it wasn't, and you were having such a good time bossing me around and making me read these books. Plus, look at you! Those motherly instincts kicked right in. You were talking about formula before the doctor even said anything. You already know more about how to take care of your baby than I could ever teach you. It's been a million years since I did this. YOU trust YOUR instincts."

---

* They had babies at the same time...I know it's odd to breastfeed another baby, until you remember that we drink milk from cows.

"Ok, but you could have told me—" I started.

"Trust me... You're gonna lie to her too, but it's only because you love her, and you want everything for her. You're going to want to protect her from mean girls, from heartache, and from acne, but you can't. I wasn't able to protect you from everything just like you won't be able to protect her from certain things. But you can get her ready." As we sat beside each other on my bed, I realized that she wasn't just my mother but also my friend.

"By the time you realized that your breastfeeding was going haywire, you were halfway through it... And what did you do when you realized that your milk wasn't coming in? You prayed! I watched a sad, heart-broken mom go into her bedroom, and out walked a confident mother talking about formula. What was the difference? Prayer and faith. If you can give your children those tools, then they'll be set for whatever the world sends their way. It can also help them survive a crazy mother who only wants to shield them from every little thing the world has to offer."

A week later I was back in the doctor's office because an infection had opened most of my now-very-painful C-section incision, and the parts that weren't had to be reopened with a scalpel—and no pain medicine. The doctor then cleaned the wound by filling it with a salt solution, making that the single most painful moment of my life.

The days and weeks that followed were some of the worst for my body, and it's the reason our children are four years apart and not eighteen months as originally planned. My body needed to heal, and my mind had to forget. I went back to work from maternity leave still practicing "wound care." I found myself saying prayers that weeks earlier didn't seem possible.

Lord, thank you for not allowing my body to breast-feed. Thank you for knowing and loving me so well. Had I been able to feed, I would have continued breastfeeding while nursing my wound, and my body needed to focus on healing.

So, hey, Jesus, it's me! Yes, I know my mama isn't exactly telling the truth about some women not having menopause symptoms, and she knows full well that I'm going to have hot flashes, cold flashes, night sweats, and . . . chin hair?? *Please, no chin hair.* But I know that she did tell the truth about the important things, like that prayer does change things, and we should never lean on our own understanding.

4

WHERE MY HOSE AT?

Hey, Jesus, it's me. Listen, I know that the Bible says in 1 Timothy 2:9–10 that women should adorn themselves in respectable apparel, with modesty and self-control... but that doesn't mean control top, does it? You aren't saying that we HAVE to wear pantyhose, are you?

I T WAS EASTER SUNDAY. BEFORE SHE got in the car, I whispered to my husband, "Don't say a word. She's a good kid, she loves Jesus, and she makes straight As."

As our twelve-year-old daughter made her way from the door to the car, he saw exactly what I was talking about. "Got it," he said. "That's your department. If you're fine, then I'm fine."

Meg was dressed in a Lilly Pulitzer sundress, and I insisted that we add a white cardigan. We were breaking enough fashion rules without wearing spaghetti straps to worship our risen Savior. Easter Sunday pantyhose had been abandoned for bare legs, and white patent leather had been replaced with Nike Air Force 1s. Yes, tennis shoes. My daughter wore tennis shoes to the Easter Sunday service. They were pure white (traditional for Easter Sunday), and she wore them with the same pride I used to have on Easter Sunday in my white patent leather two-inch heels. She had that extra bounce in her step that every little girl gets on special occasions. She knew she looked a little more special than on most Sundays.

A small part of me wondered if I was breaking mom code by not forcing her to wear pantyhose, a full slip, hat, gloves, and carry a tiny purse to pull the outfit together. But the biggest part of me was jealous. *Look at her. Living her best life in a beautiful dress, comfortable shoes, and no undergarments to restrict her breathing within an inch of her life.* I couldn't help but think of how far we'd come since my younger days.

I grew up in the '80s and '90s, and I, like every girl I knew, had a special drawer filled with pantyhose, slips, and camisoles. I didn't have to wear them every day but always on Sunday. On Sunday, they all came on for church.

Once, in a hissy fit, I asked my mom why I had to wear all this stuff just to go to church. Her eyes shot daggers into my soul as she said, "So you don't think you should dress better for Jesus than you do for your little friends?" I never asked again. I wore the pantyhose, the slip, the *everything* to keep from getting that look.

In my earliest memories, pantyhose only covered your legs, and they had no shaping or control for the hips, belly, and buttocks. You had to buy a shaping garment that you wore along with your hose.* I remember being at our local department store where I saw a one-piece shaper, and I had to have it. That shaper would solve all of my nonexistent problems. I say "nonexistent" because my body was still forming, and no shaper was going to suddenly make it look like a fully developed body. My mother did her best to convince me of this, but she decided to let me learn the hard way. As soon as I snapped the three snaps at the bottom, I learned a valuable lesson—just because it's *not* a G-string doesn't mean it can't *become* a G-string. I had spent too many days begging for this torture device, so I couldn't let her know in the first thirty seconds that she was 100 percent, completely right. I waddled my way from my room to the den.

"Everything ok?" my mom asked.

"Yes, it's fine! I love this thing!" I waddled from the den back to my bedroom and took that torture device off, and it never saw daylight again.

I once asked my daughter what she would do if I forced her to wear pantyhose, slips, camisoles, and

---

* It might have been called a girdle, but I was too young to realize it. I knew it looked like a nude one-piece swimsuit, and it had tummy control and a built-in bra.

all the things we used to wear. Her response was as expected: "Mom, stop. Don't even joke about that."

I asked my good friend who is a few years older than me what would have happened if she had told her mother that she didn't want to wear pantyhose and a slip to church. Her reaction was just what I expected.

"Uhhh, no, ma'am. I would have never even told my mother that. It was never a question." Then she said something I was NOT prepared for. "Do you understand that when I was very little, pantyhose weren't even one-piece yet? I was a little kid wearing a garter belt to church. Can you picture all these little kids wearing garter belts? Now those things are lingerie for a wedding night."

After we stopped laughing, she went on to explain that actual pantyhose were such a godsend since they were one-piece, and she wouldn't dare complain about wearing them.

It never occurred to me that there was something worse than pantyhose. Something so terrible that you were thankful for pantyhose. How far back did these things go?

I thought we wore the undergarments because our grandmothers wore them. In my mind, they wore them in the '50s and passed down the tradition, so now we all had to do it. As it turns out, I was way wrong. It seems that women have been wearing hose for centuries, and women have been trying to get rid of them just as long.

The first famous woman to wear hose was Queen Elizabeth I. She was gifted a pair by her "silk woman." That's right. She had a silk woman, and her job was to make dresses, scarves, robes... Nowhere in her job description did it say, *Create something so horrible that girls for century after century will suffer*, but she did! I don't blame the silk woman; she had a job to do. But Queen Elizabeth could have written a lovely thank-you note and put the stockings away, and nobody needed to know. Her dresses went to the floor; her legs were covered. So nobody knew or cared if she was wearing stockings under her dress. But no. She tried them on and LOVED them! And I'm guessing, like a girl in a new dress with pockets, every time someone complimented her dress, she'd say, "Thanks—it has hose." Then she'd lift her skirt and show her beautiful creation! Other ladies would see them and would HAVE to have their own pair.

* * *

One Sunday in the height of summer, I'd had enough. I needed shaping, but my heart couldn't take the thought of wearing a full pair of pantyhose all morning at church. I had the great idea to cut the legs off my pantyhose just below where the control top ends. I was so proud of myself until I was walking into the church and the small leg part that was left had rolled up while the top part had rolled down. The two rolls met in the middle, and it was all I could do to walk without moving so the roll didn't go below my hemline. Right leg, left leg, pray. Right leg, left leg, pray. I made it to the bathroom and stuffed my good idea into my purse.

Thankfully, an amazing entrepreneur had the same good idea but found a solution to the legs rolling up! Spanx hit the scene, and pantyhose's days were numbered. Once we realized that we could have control without the legs, it was a whole new world. She made shaping tops, so you could eat a muffin without worrying about a muffin top. Her shaping garments had everything you loved about pantyhose and nothing that you hated.

That Easter Sunday, Meg slid into the car with ease, not a care in the world about whether her pantyhose might roll down to her knees. Never had to care if her slip showed when she crossed her legs, or about how to keep her bra straps and camisole straps straight. She was beautiful and ready for church service, and that was all that mattered.

I wondered, *Could this be happening? Could it finally be over? Could this new generation of girls be the ones to put an end to the long-standing torture that is known as undergarments? What is our future going to look like with all these little girls not knowing the stress of keeping their pantyhose up and their slip down?* And I immediately knew the answer. Our future is going to look as bright as the sun.

More than wanting my daughter not to go through my same torture, I wanted her to feel beautiful and confident, not just in her clothes but in her skin. I wanted her to know that no matter the size or shape of her body, she is perfectly and wonderfully made. If she grows to have a muffin top, I hope she can proclaim with pride, "Yeah, it's because I ate the muffin."

So, Jesus, it's me. Thank you for the memories of control top pantyhose, and

For the stories about young kids in garter belts on Sunday mornings. Thank you for our mothers, who loved us enough to make sure that we were covered in every piece of underwear known to man. Most of all, thank you for this new generation of young girls. I promise mine will be dressed with self-control—just not in control tops!

5

GOD'S PERFECT TIMING

Hey, Jesus, in your perfect timing, it appears that my daughter is going to start her *lady time* at about the same time that I'm going to start *the change*. I know you said that you will never leave me or forsake me, Jesus, but my husband will. He will leave me AND forsake me, and he'll take our son with him, and they'll live a happy life on a boat until these female hormones settle down. How did this even happen? I'll tell you how it happened—you had me have this "late-in-life" baby.

I FIRST HEARD "LATE-IN-LIFE CHILD" when I was around six years old. Mama saw an old friend and introduced me and my brother, who was four years older than me. She was very nice and complimentary of Mama and us kids, but she also commented, "My goodness, your kids are so young." I remember Mom's demeanor changed a bit when she answered, "Well, I had them late in life." I couldn't tell if my mom was answering the question, ashamed that we were so young, or telling this woman to mind her own business. The best part was the lady couldn't tell either. I would later learn that that exact conversation was the benchmark of a Southern lady—the ladylike-ness in the words we use to set our boundaries. After the lady left, I asked my mom what *late in life* meant, and she said that she waited until she was much older than most women to have children. I did the math. She was twenty-four and twenty-eight when she had us.

From that day on, we would joke with Mom about having us so late in life. She was forty-six at my high school graduation, but she was never mistaken for a grandparent. She looked the same age as my friends' moms, and when she chaperoned my high school prom, she cut a rug without breaking her hip.

Tim and I were married when I was twenty-eight, and we had a plan in place: one year of wedded bliss and a baby nine months later. We would then enjoy our first child for one year, then have our second, so those kids would be exactly one year and nine months apart. Then we wanted a third child, and we would put three years between babies two and three. Oh! We also were going to have a boy, then a girl, and the third would be the tiebreaker.

We've all heard the phrase *We plan and God laughs.* I think it's safe to say—God made me a comedian.

It wasn't long after we married that my grandmother passed. It was heartbreaking to lose my grandmother but even more heartbreaking to watch my mother endure the loss. Once the funeral was over, she sank into her chair and said, "I'm sixty-four years old, and I'm an orphan." Her daddy had passed two weeks before my parents married.

The story goes that my grandfather gave the happy couple enough money to buy their first week's worth of groceries as a wedding present. He joked with my dad, "If I had known that I could get rid of her that cheap, I'd have done it a long time ago." Soon after, he felt light-headed while unloading hay, went to lie down, and quietly passed away.

My mom and her sisters carried on and were comforted that they would see their mom again, but still, the loss was hard. With Mother's Day on the horizon, I thought, *How great would it be if for my mother's first Mother's Day without her own mother, I could surprise her with news that I'm having a baby?* Yes! Certainly, that joy would ease the pain of the loss.

The months passed with no pregnancy. Mother's Day came with no elaborate pregnancy announcement, but Mom and I planned to spend the day together. Our church has a tradition where daughters wear a red corsage if their mother is living, and white if their mother has passed. My mom came to my room as I was getting ready. Holding back tears, she confessed, "I'm not ready to wear the white corsage."

I responded, "Well then, Mom, we'll end the corsages now. I never want to switch to a white one either." We hugged and cried but only enough to not mess up our faces.

I thought the worst was over, but then the pastor recognized all the mothers in attendance. My mom stood up, beaming to have her whole family with her on Mother's Day. My sister-in-law stood up holding her third, while her older two looked on. I sat in the pew and smiled at the new mothers while holding back tears. Why couldn't God give me a baby? Why hadn't it happened? If I couldn't stand, then at the very least I wanted to hear *It will be you next year.*

My sadness was quickly replaced by shame. Who was I to be sad about not having a baby? I had been trying for a few months while many women waited years for a child. Some suffered pregnancy loss, and many went through years of fertility treatments. I told myself I hadn't suffered enough to be sad. Thankfully, God clings close to the brokenhearted, and the shame was wiped away as quickly as it had appeared. God wants to heal our pain even if it is not the greatest pain ever suffered. I felt a peace that I would be a mom, and that it wouldn't be in my timing, but in God's.

I asked my husband if we could put starting a family on hold, and he agreed—but insisted that we continue to practice. In the months that followed, I understood how wise we had been to put a family on hold. My paternal grandfather passed away, Tim's uncle passed, and, to our complete surprise, his mother took ill and passed away, not necessarily in that order. Our focus needed to be solely on each other, and we learned that by leaning on each other through those hard times, we were already a family. A baby adds to a family—it doesn't start one. Our marriage had taken root, and we were building a foundation to last a lifetime.

We spent our third Christmas doing what we had done every Christmas since we were married. Our celebration was on December 23, which we called Christmas Eve Eve. We ordered Chinese food and exchanged our gifts before we packed up our car and spent the majority of our Christmas running the roads. We first drove four hours north for Christmas Eve with my family, then woke up on Christmas Day and drove five hours south for Christmas Day lunch with Tim's family, and finally found our way back home by Christmas night so one of us could be at work the next day.*

---

* Parents who don't want to travel during Christmas are considered thoughtful because they put their families first, but couples without children who don't want to travel during Christmas are being selfish and lazy.

That year I felt like it might be the right time to try for a baby again. I told Tim that if we started trying now, we could either have a new baby by Christmas, or I could be too pregnant to travel. His response was simple: "I'll meet you in the back."

This time, God's timing was more than perfect. I was no longer trying to have a baby to cure sadness, and we found ourselves at our first doctor's appointment in the spring. Our due date was early January. My husband's eyes beamed as he asked the doctor, "Can we get a note that she will be too pregnant to travel for Christmas?" The doctor laughed. I think he'd been asked that more than once in his career.

That first trimester went without a hitch. Telling my mom was one of the most thrilling moments of my life. There was no big reveal, no celebratory fireworks. Just a simple phone call. The only thing special about it was the moment I told my mom.

Most people were excited about our news, while others revealed that they had been raised with no manners. A few said they were "startin' to wonder," while others asked which one of us had the problem. There was no problem. God's timing meant that, like my mother, I'd start my family a little bit later than people thought we should.

My calculations were correct. I was truly too pregnant to travel by the time Christmas rolled around. My dad tried to call the doctor and talk sense into him. When that didn't work, he offered to pick me up in his full-size van and said, "Did you know the back seat turns into a queen-size bed? I can come pick you up, and you can lie down all the way home and all the way back. That wouldn't be the same as traveling because you'd be lying down." To sweeten the deal, he even offered to let Tim come with me. There was no way I would allow myself to be transported like a beached whale to celebrate the baby Jesus.

And so, our fourth married Christmas was spent at our house. We kept our Christmas Eve Eve tradition, and Santa visited our home on Christmas Eve to fill a stocking for our bundle. My parents started a new tradition of visiting us on Christmas Day. My mom came with a case of diapers in tow and said, "Look what Santa left under my tree!" My dad was beaming—his little girl was about to be a mom...and when he saw my ankles, he understood why travel was out of the question.

Our daughter was born, and our family grew by one. We lived those next three years feeling that our family was complete until one day, it wasn't. Meg was three when I texted my husband, "You think it's time for number two?" His response: "I'll meet you in the back."

Meg's little brother was born four years after her. Two felt like the perfect number for our family. Their age difference taught me that four years is perfect unless it's five years or two years or one year. Two is the perfect number of children unless you only have one or five or zero. I'm thankful for God's timing and the age and spacing of our children. It has proven to be the perfect combination for our family.

It's scary to imagine menopause and puberty intersecting in my home. Does insurance cover puberty damage? Will she hate me? Has an episode of *Dateline* ever started with *A mother going through the change and a daughter starting her lady time...?*

No matter the challenges, I know that my daughter came at the perfect time, and whatever challenges come with a "late-in-life child," I know that God's timing is perfect, and I wouldn't change a thing.

6

ADVANCED MATERNAL AGE

Hey, Jesus, it's me. I'm taking a pregnancy test for the third time. But I'm done...I *thought* I was done. No, I never got anything tied, and he never got snipped, but I got "the pamphlet" with baby number two, and once that happens, you should be done. How long ago was that? Eight years...If I was a geriatric pregnancy eight years ago, then how would this even work? Would they put Geritol in my epidural? Would I recover with normal moms, or would they put me in a nursing home? Am I about to set a world foot-swelling record? How did I even get here? Yes, Jesus, I know. I *can* do all things through Christ who strengthens me...But I don't want to!

WITH MY FIRST PREGNANCY, I remember getting ready for work and moving a quick load of laundry into the dryer before I ran out the door. Then it hit me like a brick wall. *Is there a dead fish in this room?* Now, I'm no June Cleaver, but I generally try not to let animals die in my house. Clothes may live on the treadmill, but nothing has ever died in my home. I went on to work making a note to check the laundry room for dead animals when I got home. As the day went on, I felt a sickness that sank deep into my soul. I didn't think anything of nearly falling asleep during the budget meeting, but when the smell of Chick-fil-A had me losing my lunch, I knew something was wrong. *Could this be? Is this it?* We had been trying, and we did want a baby, but I was not ready to take the test.

I thought, *I'm either pregnant or I have something horribly wrong with me.* I'm not talking about the flu. I'm talking about discovering a brand-new disease that they would name after me. There would be prayer chains, casseroles, and telethons in my honor. Was I being dramatic? No, this was serious.

I went to the grocery store and bought three items. A pregnancy test, an apple, and one extra-large jar of Nutella. The apple was going to be the start of eating healthy throughout my pregnancy, and the Nutella was to drown my sorrows of not being pregnant and the pending doom of the new disease I was sure to have. I took the test. One quick line, then waiting, waiting... *Is that a... Is it? It is!* A second line appeared. Pregnant! In my excitement, I had to celebrate, so I shared the news with my husband and quickly downed half the jar of Nutella.

I did the apple-Nutella–pregnancy test routine once more three years later. This time we added a boy to go along with his big sister. When my daughter was born, the doctor said, "Oh wow, you can have as many as you like," and that I had good strong lady parts. But by the time my son was born, he said, "So are we shuttin' this down or what?" I told him I wasn't sure and thought that I might want one more. He said he thought I could handle one more as long as I was pregnant by the time I left the hospital.

I wish I could say I was surprised by my doctor saying my uterus was made of tissue paper. I knew before giving birth that I was part of a dying breed—the Gen X mom with an infant. I didn't know what I was in for at the beginning of that second pregnancy, but it didn't take long for the doctor and nurses to let me know. I can still see the look on the nurse's face. She couldn't have been more than twenty-one and looked scared to death.

Her voice shook a tiny bit as she said, "I want you to know that we all really like you and think you are really pretty."

"Ok, thank you! I really like all of you too," I replied.

She continued, "So please don't be mad at me, but legally I have to give you this pamphlet."

I'm sorry. A pamphlet? Spoiler alert—NOTHING GOOD EVER COMES FROM A PAMPHLET.

There it was in big, bold letters.

SURVIVING YOUR GERIATRIC
PREGNANCY

"I'm sorry, but this can't be right. I'm only thirty-five," I told her.

"Oh, no! You aren't getting this because you are thirty-five—you are getting this because you are *going* to be thirty-six when the baby arrives" was her response.

"So my only way to avoid a geriatric pregnancy is to die..."

"Please don't think of it that way. It's just that a woman of your age—"

"Of my age?? Am I going to break a hip in child-birth? Should I start on soft foods now? Should we call in the family?"

"No, it's just that a pregnancy for a woman of your age—"

"Could you please stop saying 'for your age'? Nothing ends a compliment faster than 'for your age.' You look so good...for your age. You run so fast...for your age. You eat so much...for your age."

The pamphlet explained some of the risks of having a baby when you are older than the Crypt Keeper: C-section, diabetes, chromosome problems. What it never said was that due to my age, my ankles would swell to the size of my head, and my baby weight would hang on for dear life. If I could go back in time, I would tell my thirty-five-and-pregnant self to put down the caramel cake and drink more water.

By the time I got this pamphlet, I had already crossed the gestational diabetes hurdle and was cleared on all fronts. As for the risks to chromosomes—this baby was already so loved. However many chromosomes this baby had would be exactly how many we wanted. We never did further testing. My only hope was that this baby would be ok when he saw his old mother and even older father.

The C-section risk was not a big deal. I'd had one with my daughter, so I was expecting one regardless of my advanced maternal age. I don't mean to brag, but I have a *skinny pelvis*, which led to my needing the C-section. I was as surprised as anyone to receive this news. I was born a size twelve and had spent every Sunday hearing the little old ladies tell me that I would appreciate my birthing hips when I was older.

I planned my first pregnancy around my baby being born the first week of January: (a) It was my due date; (b) it fit into my work schedule; and (c) it was wild card weekend! Our new baby could be here in time to watch the playoffs.

I went in for what I knew would be my last weekly checkup. The doctor did his little exam and told me that he'd see me next week. I told him that he would see me next week, but we would be seeing each other in labor and delivery. "THIS BABY IS READY! THIS GOOSE IS COOKED. EVICT THIS BABY."

"You are not dilated in the least. It would take a miracle for you to be ready to deliver by next week," the doctor told me.

"Sir, I don't mean to tell you how to do your job, but this baby is ready to come out!"

Thankfully, my doctor and I had become friends over the past nine months, which was no accident; I chose the only Mississippi State Bulldog ob-gyn in Jackson, Mississippi. He was referred by my neighbor who was a NICU nurse, but what helped reassure my husband that this man knew about medicine was that he was an undergrad from Mississippi State. Never mind that Mississippi State is known for its veterinary medicine and I'm birthing a human child, not a cow...That was his top credential.

"Listen," he said, "if it makes you feel better, we can do an ultrasound today to prove to you that your baby is not ready."

"Sure," I said. "Let's do the ultrasound so we know I'm right."

During the ultrasound, the technician never showed her cards. I waited in the room for what felt like an eternity, then the doctor came in.

"Well! This never happens. You are right. Ms. Skrmetti, you are measuring forty full weeks. Your baby is full-term and ready. The problem is that you have a skinny pelvis."

"I'm sorry—what did you just say to me?"

"You have a skinny pelvis, and she can't get down the birth canal because it's so skinny."

I looked him dead in the eye and said, "I'm about to have another man's baby and here you are flirtin' with me. This is highly unprofessional."

I asked him to double-check about my hips. "Sir, I have been told my whole life that I could birth a baby with nothing more than a hard sneeze."

Well, the old ladies were wrong. I had the opposite of birthin' hips and would need a C-section for both of my pregnancies.

I was discharged from the hospital with baby number two without being pregnant with baby number three, but we were happy as a family of four. The next eight years in Birmingham, Alabama, showed me in real time why they say, "The days are long, but the years are short." We said goodbye to dear friends, made new ones, and realized that no amount of distance could get in the way of true friendship.

As the kids got older, my yearly doctor appointments were replaced by what felt like weekly visits to the pediatrician. I thought I was holding myself together well, but the first time we visited a clinic in Birmingham, I was fumbling through my purse for my insurance card when the receptionist informed me, "Ma'am, we don't take Medicare."

I found my insurance card and didn't kill her or shoot her the bird, which I felt was Christlike.

It was eight years after that geriatric pregnancy when I pulled out my calendar and started counting backward. Truth be told I couldn't remember exactly when my last *one* was. I had noticed that things weren't running like clockwork anymore, but I had also hoped that I was so busy with kids that I was getting my dates confused. No...this time was late. So late that it could almost be considered early for the next go-round.

So there I sat, waiting on the test and talking to

Jesus and asking him to please not pick me. Just as I explained that I can do all things through Christ who strengthens me, but I don't always want to, the test came back, and Jesus answered, "Fear not—it's only menopause."

CAN YOU GHOST YOUR FAMILY IN HEAVEN?

I T'S BEEN FIFTEEN YEARS SINCE I FIRST heard the word *ghosting*. My friends had been to a wedding in South Florida. For the uniniti-ated, South Florida is beautiful, sunny, and full of amazing people, but it is *not* Southern. At least not Southern in my sense of the word. The guest list was mostly New Yorkers who had realized why birds fly south for the winter.

My friends returned and shared a most amazing discovery.

PART TWO

The party was dwindling down with little fanfare, people just leaving without even a wave. My friends were stunned.

That night, we all learned the art of ghosting. And I had questions.

"They just left the party without saying goodbye?"

My friends confirmed I had grasped the situation correctly.

"Ok." I asked another question: "But did they say goodbye to the bride and groom?"

"NO!" they declared.

I kept on. "What about the parents that hosted the reception?"

"Nope," my friends said.

"Ok, but what about—"

"Ellen! They just left. One second they were at the party and the next they were gone, like a ghost."

For the life of me, I can't imagine getting away with that in my family. In the South, there is an art to everything, and that includes goodbyes. Our goodbyes can take longer than the hellos. If your goodbye is too short, then you are being rude, but make it too long and you've got to start saying goodbye all over again to the people you said goodbye to first.

Leaving early and leaving first are two different things. The number one rule is that you cannot be the first to leave a party unless you have let the hostess know that you'll be leaving early. If you have a sick family member or family visiting from out of town, then a good hostess appreciates that you've made the effort in spite of whatever else is going on and gets you out the door so fast your head will spin.

When it comes to leaving first, my uncle Jimmy is the king. As he gets out of his seat, he declares, "Y'all come go with us." When you hear him say that, you know that you only have about thirty minutes to start making your exit.

The other rule of the goodbye is that as the host, you can't just say, "Ok, bye—thanks for coming." You have to give them the first goodbye, then after they've made all their other goodbyes, you have to walk them out the door and make sure they get to the car without turning their ankle. Or in my family's case in the '80s, you sit in the car forever while your parents and grandparents go on and on for what feels like an eternity.

These long, drawn-out goodbyes used to feel like torture, but now I know that they were all filled with love. We do everything big in the South, and that includes love. If we've invited you over, it's because we want to see you and see as much of you as we can. We take you all in because we've learned as we get older that we may not get many chances to say goodbye.

So yes! Yes, you can ghost your family in heaven, but you'll be missing out on one of the best parts of being Southern.

7

CUPS AND ICE

Hey, Jesus, it's me. Listen, can you help my friend never know that she's on cups and ice because she can't cook? That's right. Her dressin' tastes like an eraser looks, and we can't take it anymore, but we don't want to hurt her feelings either. That's right. We want the friendship but not the dressin'.

THERE ARE TWO REASONS THAT A lady will be put on cups and ice. The first reason is because she can't cook, and in the South, we'd rather chew glass than hurt someone's feelings. It's much easier to ask someone to bring cups and ice than it is to tell them that they have no biscuit hand. The second reason is because she cooks TOO good. But take caution—if you are going to put a great cook on cups and ice, know that she won't go down easy.

I firmly believe that my mother is the greatest cook to ever be put on cups and ice. She is so good that when I tell people that she was put on cups and ice, they don't believe it. I'm not saying she was a big deal, but she was the *Northeast Mississippi Daily Journal*'s cook of the week.*

This way of cooking didn't happen overnight, though. She has had years of practice. She started cooking

---

* This was the newspaper that was based out of Tupelo, so being part of their paper was a big deal.

when she was barely old enough to see above the stove. Both of her parents worked, which meant that she and her brother and two sisters had chores to keep the house running. Her job was to get dinner started. The only mistake I've heard my mother make was the night she was supposed to make pork chops. There wasn't enough room for all the pork chops to fit in the pan, so Mom improvised and cut the bone out and the fat off each pork chop. She was so proud of herself that it was months before they had the heart to tell her to please never cut the bone and fat off a pork chop—ever.

My mother loved collecting cookbooks and recipes almost as much as she loved to cook. She would read her cookbooks like they were the Great American Novel. She would put the recipe together in her head and imagine it on her table. She would say, "This recipe calls for eggs in their biscuits—they look good in the picture but I can't imagine." For her, and most of her Southern sisters, a recipe is just a guide—they swap out ingredients, add things, and take others away.

....

*One thing that has stood the test of time is
that you could spend week after week making
the perfect version of a recipe, post it online*

*as "The perfect version of this recipe," and
the first comment will always be "I add a lil
Old Bay to mine" or "I do this same thing
except I add onion." Good cooks always
add their own flair to any recipe.*

There was only one place where Mom's amazing recipes weren't appreciated: her mother-in-law's.

My grandmother's approval was the one thing my mother wanted and the one thing she'd never get. There's a saying: "If I'm too much, then go find less." I think less is exactly what my grandmother wanted in a daughter-in-law. She wanted her to cook less, talk less, be less. But my mother could never do less, and I could never get enough of her. Don't get me wrong, my grandmother loved my mother, but it was in her own way. My grandmother was a great cook in her own right. Her caramel cakes were famous, and that was *her* dish. And what a dish to have!

It wasn't a series of family dinners that got my mother banished to cups and ice; it was one meal, and I remember it like it was yesterday. My mother had offered to bring her yeast rolls to save my grandmother time in the kitchen. The problem was my mother made, hands down, the best yeast rolls you've ever tasted. There was nothing wrong with my grandmother's rolls, except they weren't Mama's, and they needed salt. My mother also brushed a little melted butter on her rolls fresh out of the oven. My grandmother didn't think we needed the extra calories. I was excited to have her rolls, but my mama gave strict marching orders to not say a word about her rolls being better than my grandmother's. To do so would have been the ultimate sign of disrespect, and my mother respected her mother-in-law and her kitchen, so we all followed orders.

The meal was going great until my grandfather, unaware that there was a different roll maker in the house, said the one thing that should never be said.

"Well, Jennie Mae, I do believe these are the best rolls you've ever made."

As if that weren't bad enough, my mother, forgetting that my grandmother may or may not have had a voodoo doll with her name on it, said with pure unassuming and honest glee, "Oh, thank you! I made the rolls this time."

Oh, my poor mama thought she had finally found the golden ticket for full approval, but the opposite happened. For the next family dinner, the answer to the age-old question *What can I bring?* was met with the most unexpected answer: "You always work so hard; I think it's time for you to take a break and just come on over." My mom was so confused.

"You don't want me to bring anything?"

"You know what? We do need you to bring some of your good cups and ice," my grandmother said.

My grandmother wasn't wrong. My parents have owned a stand-alone ice maker for as long as I can remember. Them bringing ice was standard, but Grandmother was really saying, *Don't bring anything— especially your rolls.*

My mother couldn't imagine going to a meal without a dish, so she pried for anything she could bring. Finally, my grandmother said, "What if you bring a nice salad?"

My mother is a fine Christian woman, but the Lord is still working on her. When I tell you that woman brought every salad known to man, I'm not lying. I think she made up salads. I know this because I was the child labor that loaded them into the car.

Green bean salad, pasta salad, pretzel salad, layered salad, overnight salad, every salad you can imagine except the pear salad—you know, the canned pears with a dab of mayo, cheese, and a cherry on top? My mama said, "I don't love it, but I wouldn't kick it out of bed," which means if she was hungry enough, she'd eat it.

Nothing was said, but it was loud and clear. Mom would never NOT bring food, but she would leave the rolls to my grandmother.

I was home from college and had forgotten about the Great Roll Call and asked Mom why we couldn't have her rolls at Grandmother's house. She reminded me and I said, "What if I'm the one that makes them?" Our eyes locked. "You could show me how to make your rolls, and she has to let her granddaughter bring the rolls. Then, we can always say that I made them, even if it's your recipe. They'll be *Ellen's* rolls."

Mom called her house. "Before you start all of your cooking, Ellen wants to bring the rolls." As expected, there was little hesitation. "Well, I think she's ready," I heard Mom say, followed by "Even if they aren't, we'll grin and bear it." I wasn't offended. She was saying what needed to be said to get the good rolls to the family dinner.

I followed Mom's recipe to a tee, and the rolls were perfect! Again, our family was on the same page. These were Ellen's rolls, and it was no big deal. We all sat at the table, and right on cue, my grandfather said it again: "Jennie Mae, these are the best rolls you've ever made." Except this time, my grandmother grinned from ear to ear and looked right at me. "Ellen made the rolls this time; I can't take a bit of credit."

My mama tried to hold her composure, but, quicker than a hot knife through butter, she blurted, "She used my recipe! These are my rolls that you never let me bring. They taste just like mine."

"Welp! That was good while it lasted. Good job, Mom," I said, tossing my napkin in defeat.

After that meal, my mother went back on cups and ice and salads when going to family dinners, where she remained until my grandmother passed.

8

BLESS THIS FOOD

Hey, Jesus, it's me. Listen, when we say the blessing and ask you to bless the food to the nourishment of our bodies, can you please nourish other bodies? Not so much my body?? That's right—my body is plenty nourished.

YEARS AGO, THERE WAS A YOUNG mother, pregnant with her second child. It was the morning of her due date, and her husband was worried about going to his construction job. "If you think the baby is coming, tell me. Don't let me get two towns over, and then you have this baby."

"You know I would know if I was having a baby," she told him, and she convinced him to go on to work.

The husband drove forty-five minutes away from home to his job site and got his trucks warmed up and ready to work. Just as he was about to get on his dozer, a man yelled down the hill, "Lonnie! Hey, Lonnie! Your wife just called, and she is havin' the baby."

He took a deep breath and said to himself, "I told her not to do that."

What the young mother ~~didn't forget~~ forgot to tell her husband was that the line between *Is this labor or is this a hankering for pancakes?* was thin, and she did not ride it well. She had a doctor's appointment that morning, and if it was labor, it would be days before she could have a good batch of pancakes. Even worse, she might lose her hankering for pancakes. So, my mama took her chances, sent her husband to work, and enjoyed a pancake breakfast before her doctor's appointment.

As you might have guessed, it took the doctor about thirty seconds to determine that she was in the early stages of labor, but it seemed to be coming on faster than with her first. She said to herself, "Lonnie is going to kill me."

Daddy made it to the hospital just in time to see Mom and me being rolled out of labor and delivery. I was the first baby on either side of the family to have a full head of dark black hair. Dad leaned over to give us both a kiss, and Mom said, "Whose child is this?"

Dad said, "We know she's yours."

My sense of humor was a birthright, along with my love of Southern cooking. Because of my mom's pancake story, I joke that I was born loving breakfast, but I wouldn't have it any other way. Whoever said nothing tastes as good as being skinny feels* has never been to a restaurant where *mac and cheese* is listed under *vegetables*.

---

* Kate Moss said this in a *Women's Wear Daily* interview.

My mother might have been on cups and ice at my grandmother's house, but she made every meal special in her own kitchen, and she cooked every meal, while working full-time for most of my childhood. She would race in the kitchen creating a tornado, and once she was finished, she'd have country-fried steak, two vegetables, and a homemade bread whipped up and ready for her family.

Weeknights were great, but nothing compared to the holidays. In my part of the South, not many people up and moved away, which meant there was no picking and choosing which grandmother you spent the holiday with—you did both, and, bless your heart, when you got married, you did it four times. Southern graces don't count when it comes to giving up your child on a holiday. I watched my brother ~~survive~~ attend four Thanksgivings in one day for years while he and my now sister-in-law were dating and then newly married.

My mom was proud of both of them for making the effort but also realized that by the time Christmas rolled around, he was sick and tired of the traditional holiday fare of honey-baked ham, turkey and dressin', sweet potato casserole, mac and cheese, and the holiday fixin's. I think he had that meal ten times between Thanksgiving and New Year's.

*   *   *

There comes a time in every family when the torch must be passed. When the grandmother becomes the guest, and her daughter takes over hosting duties. My mother had a choice to make with her three siblings— should they all break off and do their own thing with their own kids and grandkids, or should they work a little harder and keep all the kids, cousins, aunts, and great-aunts and -uncles together? For my mother, there was no question. She loved her sisters and brother and their kids, and even if she had to work like she was running across Hell's Half Acre at Christmas, they were staying together.

Our family has a great cast of characters. There was my great-aunt Mavis, my grandmother's baby sister. I thought of her as my Southern charro. She lived in Venezuela and Turkey for a while, she had Southern charm, and she spoke perfect Spanish—at least we thought she did. When she and her son, Pedro, would come to visit, I would tell my mother, "I'm sitting at their table and not getting up until I learn Spanish."*

---

* I could be at the table and still not be fluent in Spanish, but thankfully, her family spoke fluent Southern.

My aunt Gen only lived a few miles from our house, so her family had to be there. Mom's older sister, Doris, lived in Florida, but she visited as often as she could, including holidays. And, of course, we had Uncle Joe, Mom's older brother, and Aunt Frances. Being sweet was plenty enough reason to be invited to Christmas, but Aunt Frances also made beautiful caramel cakes. When I was younger, she and Grandma Iris (her mother-in-law) would take turns bringing cakes to our special occasions. I can remember the last one she brought to Mama's was in a nine-by-thirteen pan, and not the traditional layer cake. I thought to myself, *You better enjoy this because it might be your last homemade caramel cake.*

Man Cannot Live by Cornbread Dressin' Alone

Mama knew that a Christmas turkey and all the trimmings wouldn't make anyone's skirt fly up. "Come on over to my house for turkey and dressin'" was a surefire way to hear, "We'll try and make it," which is Southern code for "If nothing better comes up, we'll be there."

Nope. This called for the greatest invention of all time—**breakfast for dinner**.

Mom made her famous chocolate gravy and used Aunt Gen's biscuit recipe. We had no need for redeye gravy or sawmill gravy, but she had it anyway. Aunt Gen brought fried tenderloins and helped with the other meats—country ham, sausage, and thick slab bacon.

I made my cheese grits, but Mom was worried that I had spent too much time south of I-20 and would make the grits too spicy. She saw me pull out my hot sauces from my luggage and said, "Ellen, we can't eat hot food like y'all do down there."

"Mom," I told her, "you are going to have to trust me on this."

I worked for Robert St. John, who is an institution in Southern cooking in Mississippi, and I learned to make grits from his head chef and my good friend, Linda Nance, and, in return, I shared the recipe for chocolate gravy.

Aunt Mavis was getting older but couldn't NOT bring something, so she brought her hash brown casserole. It was amazing but paled in comparison to the beautiful floating island she would bring to Grand-mother's. It sparkled in a cut glass bowl and was the most elegant dessert I had ever seen.

It's been over twenty years since Mom started this tradition. We've added boyfriends and girlfriends that have turned into wives and husbands and added even more babies to the family. At one point, Mom's house got so crowded that she asked if we should move the party to our church fellowship hall.

"We had cousins using the deep freezer as a table," she said, "and did you hear them complain?" We countered, "Being crowded is what makes it feel like Christmas."

Sadly, over the years, we've had to say goodbye to some of our family. My grandmother, along with her husband, has passed. Aunt Mavis moved to Florida and let her son and daughter-in-law care for her in her final years. Aunt Gen and her husband, R.L., and Uncle Joe have passed. I'm not saying that Mom is getting old, but last year she let me make the biscuits. So it may be time for the cousins to discuss if we keep this going or if we go our separate ways. I already know my vote.

So, Jesus, when it comes to that
celebration, you can bless all that food
to the nourishment of my body, because
the love in the dinner is worth every
calorie.

9

HEAVENLY UBER

Hey, Jesus, it's me. Listen, when we're reunited with our loved ones in heaven, how reunited will we be? Is that going to be a come and go? Or a come and stay? How about a heavenly Uber? Can I get one of those?

THINKING OF HEAVEN BRINGS ME great joy. Thinking of the people that I'm going to see and the hugs I'm going to get, there is no way I'll be able to sit in one place. When I get on that heavenly shore, I pray there'll a heavenly Uber.

The first person I want to see will be my aunt Gen. She was born Lilly Virginia but went by Gen, and my mother called me Little Gen most of my life because we both danced to the beat of our own tuba. Aunt Gen was my mother's best friend and older sister. She had an unmatched love for life, her family, and big jewelry. My mother was queen of the kitchen, but my aunt had one food that she'd mastered over my mother's—biscuits!

I can remember going into her house and her saying, "Ellen, get in my kitchen and get yourself a good biscuit. You poor thing, you probably don't even know what a good one tastes like." I'd walk into her kitchen and see a cast-iron skillet full of biscuits. They tasted like nothing I'd ever had in my life—a little crisp on the top and bottom, and soft as pillows in the middle. I like to have died. My aunt laughed. "You poor baby, you just eat your mom's thin little floury biscuits."

Technically, there is nothing wrong with my mom's biscuits, but to understand how hard we had it, when the frozen biscuits came on the market, my mom bought some and served them one morning. My older brother, Matthew, had one and said, "Where are these from?" and Mom said, "I made those," looking at me to see what he would say. My brother said, "You mean to tell me that you've known how to make biscuits that taste like this the whole time, and you just haven't?!"

I knew days before Aunt Gen passed that it was the end. She had a heart episode* and was unconscious at the hospital. My husband said, "Aunt Gen has so much here to live for; she's going to pull through." Aunt Gen might have had a lot of family on earth worth living for, but heaven had the one person she longed to see again: Kimberly. Kimberly was my aunt Gen's granddaughter and my first cousin's only daughter. We lost her in a hit-and-run accident that forever changed our family. From that day on, our family history was divided into

---

* In the South, we never give full details. Everything is either an episode or a spell. Episodes are longer than spells. Both can be minor or fatal.

two sections: our life before Kimberly's death and life after.

When Aunt Gen passed, we knew she had found perfect healing and was kicking up gold dust with her grandbaby.

When I think of seeing her in heaven someday, I picture her and Kimberly in the kitchen, and we'll all sit down and enjoy biscuits and thick slab bacon. There are no calories in heaven, which will make the biscuits all the more sweet.

After we visit with my aunt and cousin, I know I'll see my grandmother and great-grandmother, and for the first time, my great-grandmother will know who I am and whose I am! Because when I'd visited her in the nursing home, she didn't remember. That's why, before each visit, my mom would give marchin' orders: "Don't forget—Grandma is senile, so she won't know who you are, but you be sweet anyway."*

I know that in heaven I'll see Great-Grandma Keith, my mother's grandmother, who was already quite old by the time I was born. My grandma Iris, my mother's

---

* In the '80s, *senile* was a commonly used term for an older person who was losing their memory. I assumed that my family used the word because it was less scary than official medical terms.

mother, will make me feel like I'm her favorite just like she does with all of the cousins. I'll bake a caramel cake with my grandma Jennie Mae, and I'll see Tim's parents. I have always wondered what Tim's mom would think about Meg and Nik. I take that back—I've always known that she would have loved our kids. Neither looks like me—I was just a vessel to make little Skrmetti children. She would take pride knowing that Nik enjoys cooking in the kitchen just like her little boy did with her. She'd love knowing that Meg sold pies to buy a guitar, and that Nik once had a preschool report that read, "Ok except for saying the D-word."

After a good visit, I'll be on my way to find Ms. Judy, who was my best friend's mother and our town's favorite first-grade teacher. She was one of my many second mamas that helped raise me. Now that I'm a mom, I know that behind every great mom are about a dozen second mamas that help fill in the gaps for each other. After a hug from Ms. Judy, I'll be off to find Ms. Emma Street. Ms. Emma taught my mother math in high school and my dad at Northeast Mississippi Community College, so when I started falling behind in math, she was their first call. Ms. Emma was never married, she had blond hair, and her signature color was royal blue. I can't tell you if she ever wore makeup because blue lit up her beautiful face.

She was also a thrifty lady. A child of the Depression, she didn't let anything go to waste. Her home was lit with lanterns to conserve energy, and I did math equations on every piece of scratch paper known to man! Old shopping lists and the margins of the newspaper were plenty fine for long division. She would always give me a dime for my hard work. I know that doesn't sound like a lot, but it was the '80s, and a dime was more like...A DIME! It felt the same as a dime does now, but it was sweeter coming from Ms. Emma.

I picture that after I run into Ms. Emma, I'm sure to find more of the sweet old people from my church. I hope I run into Mr. and Mrs. Meadows—my first Sunday school teachers. I don't remember much about them except how much they loved us little kids. On special Sundays, Mr. Meadows would bring an apple and slice it with his pocketknife. And sweet Ms. Buela Jones! She was our daycare director, and she watched every single kid grow up. The first time I brought Tim to church, when the service was over, she asked him, "Are you as good as you look?" And I can't forget Mr. Phil. He lived alone, and the entire congregation was his caretaker. He walked to and from church, but if there was ever bad weather, he could count on a church member to swing by and pick him up and bring him to service. I'm not sure what the correct diagnosis was for Mr. Phil, but I knew that he was mentally disabled in some way and that he was gentle as a lamb. He sang in the choir and never missed a Wednesday-night practice, and he made sure no one else did either. You could set your clock to his Tuesday-night reminders. I can still hear the phone ringing, and, without caller ID, my mom would say, "Grab that phone; it's Phil reminding me about choir practice. Just be nice and tell him you'll tell me and thank him for calling." Sure as the world— it was always him.

These are only a handful of the people I'm longing to see. When I think of the one thing that binds these people together, I think of time. Each of these people spent time with me. My aunt in making biscuits and loving me. Ms. Emma gave up one night a week to make math less scary and spoke with me every Sunday and Wednesday night at church. Mr. Phil spent every Tuesday night making sure that our church had a full choir practice.

Thinking of these sweet people from church makes

me embarrassed at all the times I'm urging my family to run to the car to get out of the parking lot before the rush to the exit, change clothes for sports, or beat the Baptists to the buffet. What I see as talkin' after church is really fellowship, and I'm missing it. If I don't slow down, the sweet kids at my church are going to see me in heaven and tell their heavenly Uber, "Keep driving—that's the crazy old lady that's always rushing to her car."

So, Jesus, it's me. Will you please help me slow down and take more time with the people I love? Help me show the same love to my church family as the sweet people that shaped my life. I realize that no one will ever ask me to be a math tutor or to teach them how to make biscuits like my aunt Gen, but I do want my church family to know that I love them.

10

SOUTHERN FUNERALS

Hey, Jesus, it's me. Will you please make sure
my family gets me in the ground quickly?
Even if I'm breathin' but it doesn't look good,
have them go ahead and do it...I'm not
gonna know because I'm headed your way!

SOUTHERN FUNERALS ARE A SIGHT to behold, but you better look fast because they are over almost as quickly as they start. You'll still be fogging up a mirror,* and we'll call in the family and start glazing the ham. The line, from my Instagram sketch "If the Queen Died in the South," "Grandmaw's not doing too good, so I just want to go ahead and put that bug in your ear" came from years of experience. I cannot count how many times I heard that line but with different family members and loved ones.

That was your cue to start thawing food or get cooking because a funeral was headed your way. I can remember coming home from school and my mom had made four coconut cakes, four pound cakes, and who knows what else. In disbelief at all the food, I said, "What are you doing?!" That woman looked me square in the eye and said, "Someone could be dyin'

---

* Back in the old days, they used to hold a mirror under someone's nose to see if they were still breathing/alive.

right now." I thought every funeral in the South followed these same guidelines, or at least every funeral in Mississippi.

Tim and I had only been married for two years when his mother passed. I can remember the look on his face when he got the call. His mom had had a heart attack and would need a quadruple bypass, a risky surgery under normal circumstances but even more risky because she had just spent a month in the hospital with another illness.

Six weeks after her surgery, she passed away, never leaving the ICU. Watching my husband lose his mother was gut-wrenching. The weeks before she passed had been a roller coaster of emotions...She is getting better...She has pneumonia in one lung...She has it in both lungs. Finally, they had to make the decision to let her go.

When she passed, there was a sense of relief—not that she was gone, but that she was finally healed and free of pain, and the roller coaster was over. My North Mississippi brain thought, *Ok, it's Friday, so we'll have the visitation on Saturday with the funeral on Sunday.* But no...This was a Catholic funeral, not Baptist, and we were in South Mississippi, not North Mississippi.

I saw signs leading up to her passing that this wasn't going to be done the way we do it in North Mississippi. Before she passed, Tim's brother was gathering details to start writing her obituary—red flag number one. Where I'm from, old people start writing their own obituary around age sixty-five, keep it in the family Bible, and add to it as needed. Obituaries are too important to leave to someone other than yourself.

Red flag number two came when his dad said, "What are you doing? Stop doing that! In this family we do not bury the living."

Oh, in my family we absolutely DO bury the living. I'm not just talking about calling in the family while you are alive. I mean, during my grandmother Goolsby's funeral, my mother whispered in my ear, "Do you see how she has the flowers on the casket and the matching arrangements on either side on the pedestals? That's exactly what I want, except also add one of my quilts like when Mama died." Thankfully, my parents are still living, but they have let me and my brother know that they have already planned and paid for their funerals. The location, order of service, hymns and Bible verses, and who they want to preach their funerals, along with an alternate list in case they outlive the preachers.

The absolute ~~nail in the coffin~~ icing on the cake for Tim's mother's funeral was when the discussion turned to the flowers. The wake would be held at the funeral home, but the actual service would be at the church, which meant no flowers at the funeral. They believe that a funeral is a solemn occasion, and the focus shouldn't be on flowers but on praying for the deceased. I agree, but flowers, along with the food, are the standard by which all funerals are judged. We're really about to have a funeral without sprays of mums and gladiolas? No acetate ribbon? None of it.

....

I have a friend whose father passed away. I called her hometown florist to send flowers, and the florist was out of flowers. Can you imagine a better tribute than to know that so many people loved you that you ran a florist out of flowers?

....

Tim's mother passed on a Friday and his dad told us the plans. "We're going to do the funeral on Monday," he said.

Ok, this Monday is waiting a bit, but that's fine— we'll do it this Monday.

"This Monday?" my husband clarified.

"No, next Monday," my father-in-law said.

Such a joker—look at him joking through his grief.

He went on to explain, "Your mom's best friend is in Tuscaloosa this week for her daughter's wedding, and we need to wait until she is back in town so she can be there."

"Dad! That is ten days away, and it's on the twenty-fourth. We're going to bury Mom on my second wedding anniversary?"

"Son, this can't be helped. Plus, we're not *burying* your mom on your anniversary, just having the funeral. Your mom is being cremated, and we'll do that later."

I called my mother to let her know the plan.

"Ellen, I'm already loading up the car to get to Hattiesburg for the funeral. Listen, please don't think I'm crazy, but does your dad need one of those beanies for the funeral?"*

"Ok, Mom, first off [*googles name of hat that Jewish men wear in church*], it's called a yarmulke, and second, Tim is Catholic not Jewish. But hold off on loading the car. The funeral isn't until Monday."

---

* I don't have many regrets in life, but telling my mom that Dad didn't need a beanie is one of them. He would have worn one.

"Oh, ok. Well, that will give me more time to pack this freezer full of the food I'm bringing—"

"No, Mom," I interrupted, "it's next Monday."

"Ellen, you stop it! Is this some sort of Catholic thing?"

When Tim and I were dating, Martha Stewart Weddings *had an article titled "How to Plan Your Interfaith Wedding," and my mom asked if she should dog-ear it and save it for later. I had to clarify that* interfaith *is not for when a Baptist marries a Catholic. We are both Christians.*

I was starting to suspect that it wasn't a Catholic thing, or a South Mississippi thing, or her best friend's daughter getting married—it was a love thing. I don't think Tim's dad wanted her passing to be real. Where I'm from, we bury people quickly, and the mourning begins once the funeral festivities have settled. Stretching out the funeral gave a little more time before he had to face day-to-day life without her.

My suspicions that this was NOT normal in South Mississippi were confirmed when I stayed at the house to receive the food and keep up with who brought what.

Just as in North Mississippi, the food started to come almost as soon as she passed, and each dish came with the same comment: "Now, I haven't heard when the funeral will be..."

"Oh, it will be next Monday."

"Reeeeallly?" they would say. "That is so long!" I would explain the reasoning, and they would pretend to understand, but I could tell they were with me, that we should be having the funeral already.

We stayed in Hattiesburg the full ten days between her passing and the funeral. I gently floated the idea of going back to Jackson and coming back for the wake, but it was gently knocked down.

My friends would check in:

> How are you holding up?

> Fine...just listening to Streisand on a loop.

> Seinfeld???

> No—Barbra. His mom loved her, so his dad won't let us turn on the TV and he's playing Streisand records on a loop.

. . . .

I listened to Barbra Streisand and ate funeral food for ten days straight.

. . . .

Until the wake finally happened, along with the funeral. It was a beautiful service complete with bagpipes playing "Amazing Grace" as a nod to her Irish roots. And the repast/funeral meal was everything I expected from a Southern Funeral. The church provided the fried chicken. And when word got out that there was such a long break before the funeral, the South Mississippi ladies kicked their cooking into high gear. They kept a steady stream of food coming day after day, so there was gracious plenty for the visitors during those ten days and for the day of the funeral.

The morning after the funeral, the phone rang. It was my mother.

"Hey, Ellen. Listen, Granddaddy's not doin' too good, so I just want to go ahead and put that bug in your ear."*

---

* My grandfather passed a few weeks after Tim's mom. His wake and funeral were on the same day and less than three days after his passing.

11
GROW GUTS

Hey, Jesus, it's me. Thank you for the amazing mamas from the North, South, East, and West who love their daughters and get us ready for all that life will ever throw at us. I know we can't keep our mamas forever, but please let their marching orders stay with us as we navigate life without them.

A MY, YOU ARE GOING TO HAVE TO Grow Guts."

Those were the marching orders my friend Amy was given from her mother. I spent my life thinking that mamas giving marching orders was a *Southern thing*. Amy was a Jackson, Mississippi, transplant straight from Southern Methodist University, and she always talked about the time she lived in Texas. But one day, out of the blue, she up and started talking about Green Bay Packers football and said she was jealous that my college bookstore sold Green Bay Packers gear.*

"How do you know so much about Wisconsin?" I asked her.

"My mom is from Wisconsin, and that's where she and my dad met. We moved to Texas when I was little, and now they've moved back."

I was shocked. Amy had all the fine-tunings of being

---

* I graduated from the University of Southern Mississippi, where Brett Favre had been the star quarterback in his day, and he was the quarterback for Green Bay while I was there.

raised by a *Southern mama*. It goes to show that rais-
ing a child with good manners isn't just a Southern
thing—it's a good-mama thing. So for this, please know
that I'm replacing *Southern* with *good mama*!

Marching orders are the bedrock of a good-mama
upbringing. They often start with something like this:

"Let me tell you something right now!"

"Now, you listen to me, and you listen good!"

"I'm gonna say this once, and I'm not going to say it
again!" **But she would say it again...and again.**

If you heard anything like this, then you knew you
were about to be navigated through rough waters OR
you were about to be told how to act.

I got my fair share of marchin' orders growing up.
My most memorable came before my first boy-girl birth-
day party. It was at Cassie's, and Cassie's mama and
my mama were the best of friends. I felt so grown-up
going to a party where we'd have boys and I could show
off my pretty dress and fresh perm.

I was riding in the back seat on the way to the party,
and I can still see Mama's eyes looking at me through
the rearview mirror. Her speech went something like
this:

"Listen here, I want you to remember something.

Just because I'm not at this party, that doesn't mean I don't have eyes on you. All of us mamas talk, and it may take a few days, but we'll all know exactly what happens at this party, and at any party. So you mind your manners, because I may not be there, but I'll be watching."

I started the party in trouble and worked my way out by being a good party guest and making sure her parents had no clue that we were playing spin the bottle. Before that first spin, we all had to pinky swear that NO ONE WOULD TELL THEIR MAMA! In my little town, you are one prayer chain away from getting grounded until you turn eighteen.

Those mamas would start piecing stories together, and before you knew it, they'd figured exactly who did what, with who, at what time; and even if you didn't DO anything wrong, you could be found guilty by association. If your mama asked if you did something and you did do that something, then you should go on and fess up and just get in trouble for whatever stupid thing you did. No need for getting in trouble for doing something stupid AND lying about doing something stupid.

But the marching orders aren't just designed to

scare us into submission. They are meant to help us navigate life when we are older. When times are hard, and our moms aren't there, their marching orders are what we can lean on. And that is exactly what Amy's mom did for her.

Amy and I started as competitors in advertising sales, then we were colleagues, then competitors again, but we were always friends. We aren't opposite in every way, but in some ways we are. I'll dance into a room while Amy glides in elegantly, Amy listens better than I talk, and I still bite my nails while Amy has her nail polish collection arranged by color.

Our biggest difference is our football teams. Amy loves the Packers, and I love the Saints, but I also believe that Saturday is the best day for football. I don't think Amy has a college team, but Jesus takes all kinds.

Amy also loves Carrie Underwood—and I mean LOVES her. She has seen her live over twenty times and knows all the tricks to make it to meet and greets. The Carrie Underwood fan hierarchy goes like this:

- Amy
- Superfan

- Ultimate fan
- Regular fan

When the second stop on Carrie's Cry Pretty Tour was in Birmingham, Alabama, I sent a text to Amy that said, *I'll go with you if you want to come here.* She got the tickets to the concert but not the meet and greet. I didn't care. It had been three years since I'd seen Amy, and getting to see her was enough for me. Since I'd moved away from Jackson, we'd stayed close through text, phone, and memes, but nothing compares to seeing your friend in person.

Before the show, I asked her, "Ok, tell me what you love so much about Carrie Underwood."

She said, "I really can't explain it. Something about her music has helped me through my mom's illness."* Amy also shared the story of Carrie being scared for her *American Idol* audition and her father offering to turn the car around and go back home. "I think," Amy said, "she could have turned that car around and none

---

* Amy's mother had been diagnosed with Alzheimer's years prior. Amy would make the trip from Mississippi to Wisconsin as often as she could, and each trip, she could feel her mother slipping further and further away.

of this would have ever happened. But she grew guts, and that's the one thing my mom always told me to do—Grow Guts."

Before the concert, she asked about my Meg and Nik, and I asked her what she thought about kids. (We are close enough that I can get in her business without *getting in her business*.) She told me, "I've done the math. If I were to have a child right now, then that child and I will have the same age difference as my mom and me. I can't take the risk of putting a child through what I've been through." She went on to explain that she doesn't blame her mom at all. "The difference is my mom never knew that Alzheimer's could happen, but I do. I know it's a real possibility." In that moment, we were two mothers talking. Amy had the greatest love of a mother I have ever known.

The concert started, and Carrie did not disappoint. I started singing every single word to every song, and Amy joked, "I thought you weren't a Carrie fan!"

I made it clear: "I'm a fan. I just can't beat you in the fandom category."

Carrie played her hit song "The Champion," but it was a slightly different version than the one on the radio that featured Ludacris. For her live show, Ludacris had been replaced by a mom whose child was a patient at Children's of Alabama Hospital. The mom was a "champion" for her son and the other kids in that hospital, and she wowed everyone onstage by singing the Ludacris rap in honor of her sick child. Carrie let the crowd know that at each stop on her tour, she'd be inviting a new "champion" in each city.

I saw Amy's eyes light up. "I'm doing that!" she said.

"Amy! Are you serious?"

Amy researched and saw that Carrie would be performing in Milwaukee, Wisconsin, Amy's real hometown. She sent in an audition video, and in it she said, "I want to be my mother's champion and be the champion for all people battling Alzheimer's." She went on to explain that her mother always told her to "Grow Guts," and even though she was nervous, she was going to Grow Guts and do this for her mother!

To our shock, Amy was picked! But to no one's surprise, Amy nailed the part and celebrated her mother! Yes, my girlfriend got onstage with Carrie Underwood!

Soon after the show, Amy visited her mother at her care facility. She showed her pictures of the night and shared with her how her little girl had followed her advice and grown guts. Amy's mother couldn't understand what her daughter had done in her honor, but long before Alzheimer's took her, she knew that she had raised a little girl who had grown guts. And isn't that what all great mothers do? Prepare our children to thrive long after we've gone.

12

ALL BECAUSE OF CARAMEL CAKE

Hey, Jesus, it's me! Listen, can you please make sure that everyone fortunate enough to still have their mothers and grandmothers gets over to their kitchen right now and learns to make all of their special dishes? That's right—they need to watch them and record them because a recipe isn't enough.

I REMEMBER IT LIKE IT WAS YESTERDAY. I called my dad to shoot the breeze, but he couldn't talk. "Where are you, Dad?" I asked.

"I am under my mother's house."

"Dad, is that some Southern saying that I haven't heard yet? You aren't really under your mother's house."

We love a good euphemism in the South: *Under your mother's house* could just as easily mean in trouble with your mother, busy running errands for your mother, full from your mother's cooking—any of these would make more sense than my dad actually being under her house.

"I wish it was, but I'm actually under my mother's house." The tone in his voice let me know that he was none too happy to be under his mother's house.

"It seems my mother made the mistake of teaching my aunt Lena how to make her caramel cake, and since no good deed goes unpunished, Aunt Lena entered her caramel cake in the county fair. In a crazy twist of fate, she took the blue ribbon, which means my mother took whatever is not blue for the first time in her life."

"Ok, but how does that put you under the house?"

"Well, my mother didn't take the snub lightly, so she asked the judges to explain how they came to their decision, and the judges explained that both of the icings were perfect with the ONLY difference being that Aunt Lena's layers were more even than my mother's. So, here I lie, in the Mississippi heat, making sure that the floor under her oven is level."

"All because of caramel cake," I said, laughing.

He moaned back, "All because of caramel cake."

Every church in every town has at least one Caramel Cake Lady. You are blessed and cursed if your church has two, and heaven help you if you have three. There's an unspoken rivalry that happens between Caramel Cake Ladies that you may only notice if you are directly related to a Caramel Cake Lady. Those on the outside live in a world of bliss where there are always two or three caramel cakes on hand at church functions so there is plenty to go around, but we insiders have had conversations like this:

"Did you get a piece of my cake?"

"You know, yours was already gone so I had to try someone else's—I'm not sure whose it was." (I knew exactly whose it was—it was Ms. Mary Claire's, and hers was amazing and tasted just as good as my grand-mother's, if not better, but I wasn't crazy, and I wanted to remain among the living.)

"You poor thing. I knew I should have brought two. You know she starts with brown sugar? Or at least that's what I think she does—I haven't had enough of hers to be able to tell EXACTLY what she does."

Those few words, when pieced together, said nothing bad and everything hateful all at once. To be fair, a bet-ter granddaughter would have said, "Your cake was all gone, and I'd rather chew glass than eat anyone else's caramel cake."

While there were a number of Caramel Cake Ladies in our church, I do believe my grandmother was the most famous. It was probably because she was so will-ing to share her talent at every church function, and she hardly let a person's birthday pass without bring-ing them their own special caramel cake.

One day, I got the dreaded "Grandmaw's Not Doin' Too Good" phone call. Tests were run, and for a moment we thought it was her gallbladder. Take it out and get our ageless granny home. We weren't so lucky. Grandma had survived two bouts of breast cancer. She had a mastectomy with each one, which removed the cancer, and no further treatment was needed. The cancer had returned, but this time in her bones. It would have been easier for the doctors to tell us where the cancer wasn't rather than where it was.

My dad was tasked with telling his mother the news. Her response to her son was what I think any child would need to hear in the moment they have to start saying goodbye to their mother. She said, "There are things in life we cannot change and that we must accept, and that goes for both of us."

Now, before you think I'm letting this story get too sad and dark, let me assure you—the last two weeks of my grandmother's life were two of the best she had known. She was moved to comfort care at the hospital and was still very much in her right mind. Friends and relatives from all over came to visit. She got to tell everyone how much she loved them, and they got to tell her the same in return.

Meg was just a baby when we made the trip from Jackson to Tupelo to visit. As soon as we arrived, Meg was surrounded by cousins who played with her while we went into Grandma's room. The first thing out of my grandmother's mouth when she saw the both of us was, "Where's the boss?" and we knew she meant our

Meg. We had a great last visit, and I did ask one final burning question: "What about your caramel cake? I'm not sure I remember."

"You are fine," she assured me. "The recipe is at my house, and you'll get it. Remember, it took me seventeen tries to get it right." I had always heard that. Years ago, I spent an afternoon with my grandmother, and she showed me every step involved in making her caramel icing. I even went home that night and made a batch to make sure that I remembered my teaching. I did, but I never made it again, because I didn't have to. My grandmother was the Caramel Cake Lady!

Her funeral was exactly what you would expect after a life well lived. There were four preachers, and each mentioned being blessed by her caramel cake. The photo carousel of her family and friends featured caramel-cake photos, and, as you can imagine, there were questions.

"Can anyone make her caramel cake?"

"Who's gonna make her cakes?"

I heard my dad say, "Ellen says she knows how."

"Yes," I replied. "I just need to get the recipe from her house."

We went to her house after the funeral, and I found

her red notebook that held the caramel cake recipe. To my surprise, inside the notebook was more than one recipe for caramel cake. There were many of them—written on yellow legal-pad paper, recipe cards, and scratch paper. The ONLY thing the recipes had in common was that each was different.

That Sunday at church, people came up to my mom and gave her the recipe my grandmother had given them. Each with the same explanation: "This is the recipe that Ms. Goolsby gave me for her caramel cake. I never could get it to work, but maybe you can." My grandmother had given each person a different reason as to why their caramel might not have worked. "Cheap sugar is cheap for a reason" was my personal favorite, followed by "You're supposed to stir the mixture until your arm wants to fall off, then give it seventeen more stirs."

So many recipes, and I knew that none of them were right. Had we misjudged my grandmother? Had she been running around passing out the wrong recipe to keep everyone off her trail?

My grandmother wouldn't have passed out the wrong recipe to keep her Caramel Cake Queen status intact. Would she?

That didn't sit right. She showed me how to make

her cake. Yes, I'm her granddaughter, but I have a BIG mouth! I had the potential to tell the world about her caramel cake, put it in a book even. She had also shown Aunt Lena how to do it and still loved her after she took the blue ribbon in the county fair. Then one day, we got a letter from a friend from church.

Martha,

I'm so sorry for the loss of Ms. Jennie Mae. She was always such a sweet lady and someone I loved seeing at church. I'm sure you all have her caramel cake recipe, but I want to share with you my experience making caramel cake with her. I had asked her if she would teach me how to make her caramel cake, so she invited me over to her house where she showed me every single step, and I made sure to write everything down. I have included the steps below.

After we made the cake, we had a nice visit and she insisted that I take the cake we made home to Jack and my family. I told her that her time had been present enough, but she insisted. I so enjoyed our visit and will miss her.

Love,
Bonnie

And then it all made sense. My grandmother wasn't giving out the wrong recipe to be deceptive. Her recipe only made sense when you were at the stove making caramel icing with her. Grandmother would have happily given her recipe to anyone—her sister-in-law, her granddaughter, or a friend from church. All she needed was your time.

Hey, Jesus, it's me. Thank you for sending Ms. Bonnie to learn how to make caramel cake with my grandmother, and for giving her the good sense to take good notes. I know that my grandmother only knew the recipe while standing in front of her stove and that she loved spending time with everyone, and I know that all because of caramel cake.

13
RECIPES

THESE RECIPES ARE FROM MY MOTHer's collection of recipe cards. Before we had the Internet and twenty-four-hour cooking shows, women shared recipes through their recipe cards. Space was limited on these treasured cards, so women only wrote the key ingredients and made the instructions as precise as possible with the understanding that the recipe was being handed from one Queen of the Kitchen to the Other.

They aren't for the faint of heart, and you need to bring your own set of cooking skills. I once used a recipe and said, "Mmm, this recipe doesn't call for salt," and Mama replied, "Now you know that recipe needs salt."

Mama's Yeast Rolls

3 packages of dry active yeast

½ cup warm water—let the yeast sit in water while you mix up rolls

1 cup boiling water

1 cup Crisco

⅔ cup sugar

Mix together to melt Crisco

Add:

1 cup cold milk

2 eggs

2 cups plain flour (5–6 cups in all)

1 T. salt

Mix well then add the yeast mixture and additional flour to make a soft dough. It will stiffen when it chills.

Cover and let rise for one hour. You can either refrigerate to use later or go ahead and roll out and let rise again and bake at 400 degrees until brown as you like them. The dough will keep 3–4 days in the refrigerator. Take out 2–3 hours before you need them to allow plenty of time to rise.

My Grandmother's Caramel Icing

These instructions came from Ms. Bonnie, who wrote them down while watching my grandmother make this icing. I promise if you have an ounce of kitchen skills and you can follow this recipe, then you'll have caramel icing. But if you try and fail and fail again, then you understand why old Southern ladies guarded their recipes. We can't all be Caramel Cake Ladies.*

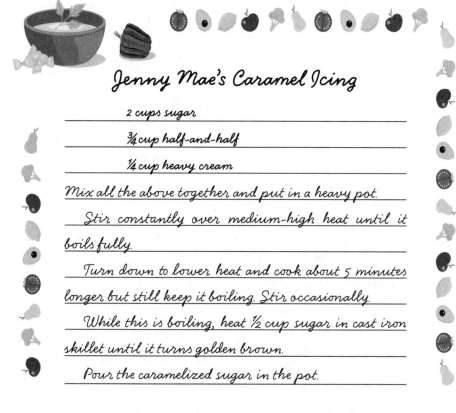

Jenny Mae's Caramel Icing

2 cups sugar

¾ cup half-and-half

¼ cup heavy cream

Mix all the above together and put in a heavy pot.

Stir constantly over medium-high heat until it boils fully.

Turn down to lower heat and cook about 5 minutes longer but still keep it boiling. Stir occasionally.

While this is boiling, heat ½ cup sugar in cast iron skillet until it turns golden brown.

Pour the caramelized sugar in the pot.

---

* The ladies know it goes on a yellow cake and nobody cares if it's a box mix because the icing is the star of the recipe.

Add 1 stick butter and continue to stir about 5 minutes until it coats a spoon.

You can also check by putting a small amount in cold water and see if it balls up.

Let it stay on the burner and stir a little longer.

Set the pot in a sink with shallow cold water.

Add 1 tsp. of good vanilla.

Stir until cool and spread on cake.

This only takes 20 stressful minutes.

Gen's Biscuits

2 cups self-rising flour
1 stick butter plus extra for the pan
Buttermilk (about 1 cup)

Preheat oven to 450.

Melt a few tablespoons of butter in a cast-iron skillet.

Cut butter into flour, add buttermilk to make a soft dough. Roll and cut out biscuits. Place in the skillet turning each one to get butter on the tops of the dough. Bake at 450 for 10–12 minutes until light brown. Gen always teased me: Because I don't turn my biscuits in the butter my poor family has to eat floury biscuits.

Mama's Chocolate Gravy

2 cups sugar

⅓ cup cocoa powder

Mix well and add:

½ to ⅔ cup milk

Bring to a rolling boil then add:

1 stick of butter

1 tsp. vanilla

Serve over hot buttered Biscuits.

I'D RATHER CHEW GLASS THAN TALK UGLY ... BUT CRUNCH, CRUNCH— HERE WE GO

PART THREE

I'D RATHER CHEW GLASS THAN TALK *ugly, but crunch, crunch—here we go.* I'll never forget the first time I heard those words or who said them. It was my coworker Justin Jordan in the Crescent City Grill during cash-out.* The moment I'd walked through the doors of the Grill, I knew I'd found a group of folks like me.

I'm a proud community-college kid, so by the time I got to a four-year college, the sorority life was out of the question. I was sharp enough to know that I could never be the junior who gets into a good sorority. It was fine, though. I graduated from the University of Southern Mississippi. I broke my daddy's heart when I didn't go to Mississippi State, but he had two criteria for choosing a senior college: (1) He wasn't paying out-of-state tuition; and (2) he wasn't paying private-school tuition. He thought that meant Mississippi State was locked in, but I found a loophole in Southern Miss. It was four and

---

* Cash-out happens when the waitstaff turn in their receipts, cash, et cetera, before they leave for the night.

a half hours away, and South Mississippi felt like a different state than North Mississippi.

I finished my two years at Southern Miss and didn't want to leave. I made a few right turns in life and ended up working for Robert St. John. In Mississippi, Robert is an institution, a fierce supporter of eating local, buying local, and living local. In the early 2000s, his restaurant on Hardy Street in Hattiesburg, Mississippi, was three restaurants in one. The Mahogany Bar was in the middle. The Crescent City Grill, the casual-dining restaurant, was on one side, and the Purple Parrot, the fine-dining restaurant, was on the other.

Robert created something special in that building. We were a family. In the restaurant business, there's often a line of demarcation between the front- and back-of-house staff,* but not there. We worked hard, but we worked together.

That restaurant became my sorority, and everyone in that building became my family. Justin stayed, worked hard, and is now a general manager and full-fledged member of the St. John family. I, on the other

---

* Front-of-house is everyone you see in the dining room while back-of-house is everyone behind the scenes making sure you have the best meal of your life.

hand, started dating a customer, fell in love with the customer, and then followed that customer all over the South. Of course, I'm joking. I don't regret a single step in my journey. I would leave again, but I'd work there a million times over.

It's been over twenty years since I worked there, and we still keep up and support each other. We cheer when one of us wins, and we mourn when one passes. The Crescent City Grill was and still is a special place. It's the home to the best corn-and-crab bisque in the world, the famous Sensation Salad, and the birthplace of *Crunch, crunch—here we go!*

14

THROW STONES

Hey, Jesus, it's me. Listen, I know that they say people in glass houses shouldn't throw stones...Ok, well, how about this rock? Can I throw this rock?

MY PAGEANT DAYS WERE SHORT but I have great memories. I begged my mom to let me compete in our Miss Tippah County pageant. It was a preliminary to the Miss Mississippi pageant. I told my mom, "Mom, I think I can win Miss Tippah County, and I want to see what Miss Mississippi is all about." She was worried about the time it would take to get ready for Miss Tippah, and, heaven forbid, what if I won both that and Miss Mississippi and needed to prepare for Miss America?

"Mom," I told her, "I'm a rookie. No rookie has ever won Miss Mississippi, but I do want to go and see what it's like and see if I can hold my own."

"Why not wait until next year when you aren't so busy?" she asked.

"I think it would actually be easier to do it this year when I *am* so busy."

> *Real talk: I pushed to do it that year because I was skinny NOW and I needed to make the most of my metabolism.*

Mom agreed to let me enter the Miss Tippah County pageant, and by the time I won, she could have been a certified pageant pro. She had her sights set on Miss Mississippi. She had researched and knew who was the best at everything. My evening gowns came from Ann Northington, who dressed the current Miss Alabama turned Miss America. "There is a lady in Vicksburg that makes everyone's swimsuits," she said. "She even has four-ply tummy control."

"Are you saying I'm fat?"

"No. But if you can buy a swimsuit with four-ply tummy control, then you buy the swimsuit with four-ply tummy control." *Now, those are words to live by!*

"Oh, and I talked to Ms. Brenda, and her daughter JJ is coming over to show you how to use Firm Grip on the bottom of your swimsuit so your suit doesn't ride up and packing tape on your top so your cleavage looks nice and full."

Brenda is one of my mom's closest friends, and her daughter was our former Miss Tippah County Hospitality. Jennifer Joe (JJ is what we called her) taught me everything I know about Firm Grip, boob tape, and the pageant wave.

"Now, Ellen," JJ cautioned, "you're going to need to make friends at this pageant because you need one hand to pull the swimsuit over a buttock, another hand to spray and fan it dry, and another to get it ALL THE WAY BACK UNDER your butt so it sticks right. You find the nice girls because the last thing you want is to let a mean girl back there, spraying too much, and you can see the sheen in the stage lights—or even worse: they put on too little and your suit rides halfway up your butt cheek while you're onstage. You'll never live that down."

She was right. There ain't enough daddy's
money to stop that gossip from spreading from
generation to generation. I can hear it now ...
Welcome to Ole Miss Rush! Isn't your mom the
girl whose swimsuit rode up her butt cheek
at Miss Mississippi? Yes? She is? You are cut.
Thank you for playing.

"Now, are you ready to learn boob tape?" JJ continued.

"Oh, JJ, what have I gotten myself into? I am an idiot for thinking I could do this."

"You are not," she said firmly. "This is the life of a pageant girl. We are all just blush, boob tape, and butt grip, and the key is to smile and make it all look natural ... in four-inch heels."

To my surprise, each girl competing was nicer than the next. We were all on this journey together. Especially during the swimsuit competition. When I think back on it, I only see hands.

After we rushed backstage, we had exactly two minutes to change into our swimsuits. I started by bending over so two other girls could try to make cleavage out of what skin and fat I had. One girl pushed my right boob to the middle while another pulled my left boob to the middle. Then I pulled the tape across the side of my back all the way under the bottom of my boobs and voilá—I looked up and there stood Dolly Parton in a red swimsuit. There was no time to revel in my new cleavage, though. We had to Firm Grip my butt, then help the other girls.

In two minutes, we were all taped and gripped to perfection. And that could sum up the week. Each girl was as beautiful on the inside as the outside. We weren't competing with each other, only trying to be the best version of ourselves.

As expected, I didn't win Miss Mississippi, but I did win some great friends and the occasional opportunity to judge other pageants. I had cousins who lived just north of us in West Tennessee. Their local high school called and invited me to judge their beauty review, and I accepted. It was one last chance to throw on my crown and heels.

This pageant took place in the school's large gymnasium. There was no "backstage," so the audience could see the girls as they lined up and waited their turn on the runway. The girls probably didn't realize it, but I paid as much attention to how they interacted with each other before they hit the stage as I did to when they walked the runway.

I zeroed-in on one contestant who had professionally styled hair in a French twist, perfectly rolled bangs, and a strategically placed ringlet of hair on each side of her face. I could tell that her makeup was professionally done, and she'd paid God only knew how much for her sparkling dress. Technically she was beautiful, but the glares she gave the other girls dimmed every sequin and rhinestone on her dress. She hit the runway, and her family yelled her name. I caught her little eye roll that she quickly turned into a pageant smile.

Then another girl caught my eye as she stood ready for the runway, smiling and talking to the girls on either side of her. She'd only taken a couple of steps when her family clapped for her, but that was drowned out when the student section raised a raucous cheer. In all of that noise, she tried to keep a straight face but failed. She started to laugh, which only made her even more beautiful. This girl was the exact opposite of the one before her.

I noticed that her evening gown was handmade or a hand-me-down, but the beautiful chiffon matched her olive skin. Her hair was in a simple chignon, but simple was making a comeback in the pageant world.

There were two people judging with me, and we all had to agree on a winner. There was a tie. Wouldn't you know it, Miss Sequins and Miss Sunshine were in a dead heat.

The three of us judges now had to share our opinions about who should win. When they asked for my opinion, I said, "I say we let the sequins break the tie. Those are pretty, but the trend is going toward less sparkle. The other girl is very on trend with her hairstyle."

"Really? I didn't realize," one of the judges said.

"Oh yes—simple is definitely the way to go with pageants these days," I said, flying high on haute couture.

"Well, I guess that settles it."

The emcee announced the third and second runners-up, and it was down to Sequins and Sunshine. Whichever name wasn't called next would be the winner. They crowned Miss Sunshine as Miss Whatever, and I skedaddled out of there as fast as I could.

I made it over the state line and back home in time for supper, but the news had beaten me home. "What happened at the pageant?" Mama asked before I could make it all the way in the door.

"Well, the good news is that the perfect girl won, or at least in my eyes. The bad news is we may never be welcomed back to that town again. There was just something about the girl that won. I wanted her to win so bad."

"Well, honey, I couldn't be prouder. That was your aunt Gen on the phone. The girl you picked is one of the sweetest girls in town, and she's been having a tough time, but you made her day. Her family didn't have a lot of money, but they did the best they could for her pageant look."

"Mom! I can't explain it, but I just felt like that girl had to win." It made no sense, but it had to be her.

"It was probably the Lord using you to help make someone's day brighter."

"Mom, stop...It wasn't that."

"I'm serious," she said. "He has no other arms but ours, and no other voice but ours. He used you to help her feel better."

If that's the case, then, Jesus, you go ahead and let them throw all the stones they want, because I'm safe under your protection. Help me to never fear the stones that others may throw, because I don't live in a glass house. I live under your loving arms.

15

BAD APPLES GIVE GOOD ADVICE

G IRLS... I'M SORRY, GIRLS... CAN YOU please gather around here for a second? Please! This is important and I can't let this slide."

Ten minutes into our first practice for Miss Mississippi, and we were already getting a come-to-Jesus.

"Ladies, this is the Miss Mississippi pageant, and ONE of you will win, which means you will be Miss America or in the TOP TEN at a MINIMUM. Now, I cannot tell you who is going to win, but I can tell you this: The winner will not be wearing a square heel!"

"You! Miss Magnolia!" he yelled. "Come up here, please."

Miss Magnolia stood next to him. "Ok, look at her leg. Long and lean with an invisible line to the floor."

He pointed to another contestant. "Now...you... I'm sorry to call you out but look at this square heel! And I know you thought that getting a shade that matches your pantyhose was the way to go, but it is not."

He turned back to Miss Magnolia. "Look at her leg in comparison to Miss Magnolia's leg...Which leg do you want?

"Ladies, long story short, you need four-inch acrylic heels if you want to win this pageant. I call them pageant heels; others may call them stripper heels. If you can't find any, I suggest you go where the strippers get their heels, and you will find gracious plenty."

I leaned over to the girl next to me. "Who is this person?"

She shushed me before she said, "He is the choreographer, AND he was the apple from the Fruit of the Loom commercials."

"You stop!" I exclaimed. *Those Fruit of the Loom commercials were famous.*

"Yeah, he was the apple AND he was Little Ricky's best friend in *I Love Lucy*."

146

And that is when I knew I was about to be on the adventure of a lifetime.

I might have thought I could win Miss Tippah County, but I knew that I was going to Miss Mississippi for one reason and one reason only—to observe and report! There were girls—and Lord bless them for it—who were there for the sixth time trying to make it to the Miss America pageant. I knew that I was a one-trick pony, so I watched every single moment and took in every piece of knowledge I could.

There were the fancy girls from Jackson who had debut balls and private schools. Their Junior League mothers raised them on the art of china patterns and Southern graces. I think those girls came out of the womb walking gracefully.

Not me. I had Martha Goolsby and a camcorder. She would record my walk and play it back: "Look—see? Your arms are swinging when you walk. You need to hold your shoulders back and you need to learn to walk in these stripper heels like they are house shoes."

"Mom, where did you find these?"

She told me, "Don't ask," so I never did again. But when I got home from school, I immediately took off my school shoes and wore high heels until bedtime.

She also made sure I held my own in my interview. "Ellen, you need to be able to carry conversations with anyone and not be intimidated, so I have arranged for you to meet with the most intimidating woman we know, and you are going to talk with her until you feel comfortable in every room." I knew exactly who she was talking about—my great-aunt Doris. She was my grandfather's older sister. Until she passed, she carried herself with an unmatched grace.

Great-Aunt Doris was serious about these chats. Each week she clipped the biggest articles from the state and local papers, and we would discuss each one. I learned so much from her, but the best thing she ever told me was to always keep one hundred dollars in my sock drawer in case I needed to get out of town, and if my husband ever said, "You don't make bread like my mama," I should tell him, "You don't make dough like my daddy."

Hairdressers and makeup artists aren't allowed backstage, so every girl had to do her own hair and stage makeup. I met with Ms. Sherri Bullard* every

---

* Every special occasion, Sherri wore a hat the size of Texas and was the only woman in town that could pull it off. She could wear every color in the color wheel, and her long brown hair would flow from

week at her Merle Norman studio for makeup lessons. Sherri is one of the colorful Southern characters that every small town needs. The only thing bigger than her hair was her heart, and she always had a story about some crazy adventure she had gotten herself into. You might have had a Merle Norman in your town, but you haven't lived until you've been to Ms. Sherri's Merle Norman studio. She named hers Merle Norman and *More*, with an emphasis on the *more*. In the '80s and '90s, her studio was a proper ladies' dress shop with the makeup tucked in the corner, and today, she and her daughter Natalie run the transformed store as one of the largest prom and pageant stores in the country, with the makeup still tucked in the corner.

After months of preparation, it was time for pageant week. There was one girl competing with us who might have been the only first alternate who had to perform the duties when the winner of her local pageant couldn't. The winner of her pageant was in an unfortunate situation, and she knew that once everyone knew about her unfortunate situation, she could never do

---

under the hat. One Easter Sunday, she was late to church, and when they sat down, her husband whispered, "We had to kill the bird," referencing the feathers on her hat.

another pageant. But she just had to know if she could win her local, even if it meant not being able to move on to Miss Mississippi later.

> *I'm still in awe of the winner. She could have*
> *had her situation taken care of, joined us at*
> *Miss Mississippi, and we would have been*
> *none the wiser. But she chose life, and all the*
> *gossip that comes with it in a small town. It's*
> *a reminder that being pro-choice also means*
> *being anti-gossip and pro-mother.*

Once the pageant had gotten underway and all us girls were getting to know one another, I commented to one contestant how nice the outgoing Miss Mississippi was, and another girl answered, "You know she smokes." She was either jealous or from Jackson.

During a break, our conversation turned into how trashy Miss USA was in comparison to Miss America. This was 1995, and Miss America was still THE PAGEANT to win. It aired during prime time and on one of the big stations (which meant you could find it on the dial of your TV).

"If you really want to be in a national pageant," the

girl said, "Miss USA has no talent, but you have to wear a two-piece swimsuit. You don't actually have to, but most of the girls do, so you'll look like a granny if you wear a one-piece." *I'll take voice lessons and a one-piece. I'm not doing a two-piece unless it comes with a biscuit.*

Another girl chimed in: "You could also figure out how to do one of the other state pageants. Not Georgia, Alabama, or Tennessee, or any of the states around here," she quickly clarified, "but out west..."

"Oh yeah," another girl said. "I heard that some of those state pageants only have like twenty girls in them, and I think any one of us could win."

Not this girl. My pageant experience can be described as "Here for a good time, not a long time."

But the best moment of all—the one I will never forget—was THE PIZZA! God bless the Miss Mississippi organization! The night the pageant aired, they announced the top ten finalists that had been compiled from our preliminary nights. Those ten would compete in talent, evening gown, and swimsuit while the rest of us...ate pizza!

Piping-hot loser pizza was waiting for all of us who didn't make the cut! It was amazing. I think some of the girls were in denial that they were eating loser pizza, but they shouldn't have been. From the beginning, it was a two-horse race, a competition between Kari Ann and Monica. They were both as kind as they were beautiful and had talent to spare. They both had grace and confidence that only come with experience.

We put down our pizza long enough to perform our dance numbers and watch the winner get her crown. As predicted, it came down to Kari Ann and Monica, who were holding hands when Kari Ann's name was called. Monica was the winner, and just as the apple from the Fruit of the Loom commercials predicted, she was top ten in Miss America. The following year, Kari Ann took the crown, and once again, just as the apple predicted, she was top ten.

No, I didn't win that night, but sometimes the win is in the journey. That pageant taught me that one day I'd have the grace and confidence that come with experience. When my NON-PAGEANT time came, I'd be ready. I started that pageant a scared little girl from Ripley, Mississippi, and I left knowing I could talk to anyone, how to hold my own in any room, and how to elongate my leg in a swimsuit competition. No, I didn't win Miss Mississippi, but I certainly didn't lose.

16

AN EGG BOWL FULL OF NUTS

Hey, Jesus, it's me. Listen, can you please keep Mississippi State and Ole Miss fans close to you? Well, extra close during the Egg Bowl because when it comes to that game, the whole state goes nuts.

I CAN REMEMBER THE TIME MY DAUGH-ter asked me, "Mom, what if I wanted to go to Ole Miss? Would you let me go?"

"You stop it!" I told her.

"No, really. I'm serious. What if I really wanted to go to Ole Miss? Would you still love me?" I could tell by the look on her face that she was trying to get my goat.

"Of course I'd love you, but there is no good reason for you to go to Ole Miss."

We had already moved to Alabama, so I ended the conversation with this: "Between Mississippi State and the in-state tuition you get from Alabama and Auburn, every possible area of study is covered. There is no good reason for you to go to Ole Miss other than to hurt my feelings and kill your daddy."

I always knew that there was something special about the Mississippi State–Ole Miss rivalry, but I never could put my finger on what exactly made it special until I traveled to California. I knew I was from a small part of the world, but it didn't hit me how small until I traveled to Napa Valley for the first time. After my plane landed in San Francisco, I rented a car for the rest of the journey. Along the way, I saw billboards. So many billboards for teams. For football, the San Francisco 49ers and the Oakland Raiders. For pro baseball, the San Francisco Giants, and for basketball, the Golden State Warriors. It made me think about Mississippi State football, and I wondered, *Would I care so deeply about my team if I had a major-league team to distract me? Would my home state be as crazy about the Egg Bowl if we had other options? What if the people of Mississippi had the option of cheering against each other on Saturday night but then joined together to cheer FOR a professional team on Sunday?* That's when I realized that our crazy is so concentrated on two college teams' rivalry that it erupts out on one night a year during the Egg Bowl.

You may ask, "Why is it called the Egg Bowl?" and I would say, "Why isn't every bowl game called the Egg Bowl?" It gets its name from the big football on top of the trophy that looks like an egg. In the "Battle for the Golden Egg," the winner of the Egg Bowl gets to keep the trophy and throw it in the losers' faces until the next game. More often than not, the game is played on Thanksgiving, when both teams take turns hosting the beautiful Thanksgiving-themed tailgates for their friends and family! I had a friend from another state ask, "Don't you want to spend Thanksgiving with your family?" and my response was, "We are." Plus, a Thanksgiving tailgate is a sight to behold. Turkey and dressin', casseroles, pies, and all the fixin's. Somewhere buried deep in a storage unit is a VHS tape of my husband and his friends lowering a turkey into a fryer on ESPN.

It's been said that Mississippi is a club, not a state,* and that sums up Mississippi in a nutshell. It's rural, and people move to the state usually for one of three things: work, family, or rehab. People might move inside the state, from Tupelo to Jackson or Biloxi to Natchez, but most of the people who were born in Mississippi tend to stay. It's not that the state won't let you leave; it's more *Why would you want to?* In Mississippi, you're surrounded by people who love you, and you get to rake up kin at every turn. (If you ever find that life is moving too fast, I invite you to take a Mississippi slowdown. Walk barefoot in the rich Mississippi Delta

---

* I first read this in a piece by Wyatt Emmerich, who publishes the *Northside Sun* in Jackson, Mississippi, and other local papers across the state.

soil, listen to some blues, or sit on a dock and watch the fresh seafood flow freely on the Gulf Coast.)

....

Raking up kin is a time-honored tradition in Mississippi. It's how we find who all we have in common. You meet someone new and find a similarity.

Oh, you're from Tupelo? My grandmother is from Tupelo.

Then we visit at Christmas, and you figure out that her grandmother's next-door neighbor was your favorite Sunday school teacher. Now y'all are like family.

....

Mississippi is on the small side, so everyone knows everyone's business. Then you go ahead and put two SEC West schools only a hundred miles apart, and you have a recipe for a rivalry that is something special. Whether the game is played in Starkville or Oxford, the homes of State and Ole Miss, respectfully, the players and fans have been going to school, church, and work together for a long time, so their only chance to outdo each other boils down to sixty minutes on the football field at the Egg Bowl. There's no Sunday game or a national championship—we have that one game, so those braggin' rights mean everything. For perspective, the only other state with two SEC schools in the same division is Alabama: the University of Alabama and Auburn. But even though the Iron Bowl is always a nail-biter of a game, the state of Alabama has more distance between the two schools and a little more good sense among the population.

I once watched the Iron Bowl with some of our Alabama and Auburn friends, and it stumped me. The game was a close one that went down to the wire, but at no time did the Alabama and Auburn fans dog-cuss each other or call each other names. In my wildest dreams I cannot picture a joint Egg Bowl watch party going that well.

Mississippians are more serious about football than their Southern graces, so my beautiful Hospitality State gets madder than a wet hen at a rivalry game. After living on top of each other for almost a year, we've bottled up so much animosity toward each other that by the time the Egg Bowl rolls around, there's a big pot of hate waiting to boil over.

Now, both schools do love their fans. All are welcome. There are many schools that use the term *sidewalk fans* in reference to people that cheer for a team but didn't attend the school, but neither of our schools would degrade their fans by putting them in that category. Our fans are divided between *uses the sense the good Lord gave them* and *half stupid.** When it comes to the half stupid, a college degree won't keep you off that list *or* get you on it. Any and all are welcome to either ring a cowbell or yell "Hotty Toddy."

You won't hear me yelling Ole Miss's famous "Hotty Toddy" cheer, because I'd be grounded if my mother ever heard me say it. Not because it's Ole Miss but because it uses curse words in the cheer. It goes like this:

> *Are You Ready?*
> *H*ll Yeah.......D@mn Right*
> *Hotty Toddy Gosh almighty who the h*ll are we?*
> *Flim Flam Bim Bam Ole Miss*
> *By D@mn!*

Ever the sophisticate, Mississippi State cheers for their team by ringing cowbells. That started with a game many moons ago when Mississippi State was

---

* We'd never call anyone full stupid or plumb stupid, because even a broken clock is right twice a day.

losing to Texas A&M and a cow walked onto the field (cows are no longer allowed on the field), and State went on to win the game. The cow was (obviously) good luck, so why not keep the luck going? Fans started bringing their cowbells to cheer on the Bulldogs.

Ole Miss is home to the law school and medical school, and they have supporters like Gerald McRaney, Tate Taylor, and Morgan Freeman. Doctors and celebrities are nice, but Mississippi State has a dairy...on campus. And not just any dairy. Mississippi State is home to the only top ten collegiate Jersey herd. When Ole Miss fans call State a cow college, State fans take pride in being one of the best cow colleges in the United States. And even an Ole Miss fan is happy to receive a Christmas delivery of Mississippi State cheese.

Because the players on both sides have spent most of high school either playing with or against each other, they know how important this one night is. They're some of the best and brightest in Mississippi who love their teams properly, and the ones that aren't from Mississippi are taught how to hate the other team during the recruitment process. The Egg Bowl has always had its share of scuffles, but during one game, the tension was so thick that you could cut it with a knife. It reached its boiling point and both teams broke into a fight at the fifty-yard line. With so many players on the field either fighting or trying to stop the fighting, the referee had no choice but to say, "Unsportsmanlike conduct on all players on both teams." When the State coach started yelling at the Ole Miss athletic director, I think ESPN had to go on to the next game. How many athletic directors get called into the SEC commissioner's office for one message? "Tone it down!"

I'm glad to say that our rivalry has toned down to the normal levels of hate and disdain. It helped that Ole Miss hired Lane Kiffin and State hired Mike Leach to lead the teams, and both coaches shared a mutual respect for each other. In 2022, Coach Leach won what we would later learn to be his final Egg Bowl and final game of his career. He passed weeks after that Egg Bowl.

In a statement on Twitter, Lane Kiffin said this about Coach Mike Leach:

> I truly loved Coach Leach and every minute I shared with him. I have been able to work with several of his former players and coaches, and they have told me so many amazing stories

about the impact he had on their lives. Going back to our years together in the Pac-12, I have always felt tremendous respect and admiration for Coach, his unique personality and his innovative mind, and I can't imagine college football without him. I'm grateful to be part of his final win, hug him and watch him walk off like the winner that he is. I know God is welcoming the Pirate home now.[*]

After a game like that, followed by those beautiful words from Coach Kiffin, you would think that the rivalry would simmer down, but this is football and it's SEC football and it's SEC football in Mississippi, and we are still looking forward to the next Egg Bowl full of nuts.

---

[*] Dani Mohr, "Ole Miss' Lane Kiffin on Death of Mike Leach: 'Can't Imagine College Football Without Him,'" *Mississippi Clarion Ledger*, December 13, 2022.

17
NAGGIN' WIFE

Hey, Jesus, it's me. Listen, I know the Bible says, "Better a man live in the desert than with a naggin' wife." So ...do I just take him to any desert? Oh! You say you'll come pick him up?

IF A MAN HAS A NAGGIN' WIFE, THAT IS a vicious cycle. Which came first—the naggin' wife or the man that needs naggin'? They probably both need Jesus and a clean slate to stop the chaos.

I've (almost) never been a naggin' wife, but I have been a mouthy one. There is nothing wrong with a woman being a little mouthy. Mouthy women aren't afraid to stand up for themselves and others, and I come from a long line of mouthy women—my favorite being my late mother-in-law! Her level of mouthiness can be summed up by one single action.

She was a naval nurse from Upstate New York who met a marine from Biloxi, Mississippi, while he was stationed on her ship. They fell in love, and he brought her home to meet his family. Everything was going great, except on this trip, he lost his Southern graces and started bossing her around. Trying to impress his family that he'd found a woman that would cater to him, he started telling her to fix his plate or take his plate. By the second day, she'd had enough, and when he told her to fix him a glass of milk, she did just that. She fixed *him* by filling a glass with ice-cold milk and pouring it right on top of his head for all of his family to see.

The room erupted in laughter, and the Yankee girlfriend got the Southern seal of approval. They were married soon after.

I recently asked Tim if there was ever a time in our seventeen years of marriage that I have nagged him. He said, "This feels like a trap, and I refuse to answer on grounds that I know better."

"I promise it's not a trap. Can you name a time that I've nagged you?"

He went on to remind me of the time I tried to get him to start a donut truck because there wasn't a good donut shop in town. Then he remembered the time I started a photo-booth business and almost worked us to death one Christmas. But what he truly loved was reminding me of our first Christmas, when I had to go out to a tree farm, and I wanted the biggest Christmas tree on the farm. He tried to convince me that it was too big for the den, but I was relentless. He let me learn the hard way that he was right. That tree gave the Griswold-family Christmas tree a run for its money.

"First of all, I said ONE time. And second, I wasn't naggin' you; that was just being mouthy. Being mouthy and nagging are two completely separate things!"

"Spoken like a true naggin' wife," he joked.

Whether you call it *mouthy* or *naggin'*, it should never be confused with *tacky*! Tacky might be the most horrible thing you can call a woman in the South. "That's downright tacky" or "You're acting tacky" or "That looks tacky" are the kisses of death. We avoid *tacky* at all costs. There's a thin line between *mouthy* and *tacky*, and the best Southern women ride it well.

Tacky is one of those words that are hard to define but easy to spot:

- Not pulling over for a funeral procession is down-right tacky. I don't care if you are on the inter-state. Someone has passed away, and we pay our respects by pulling over (and turning down the radio).

- Taking food to a widower too early is plain tacky. Ladies, I know good men are in short sup-ply, but please do not show up with a casserole and bad intentions until the grass has grown over the burial plot. I saw this happen with my father-in-law. I think the ladies waited a week before they started bringing him food. It beat all I'd ever seen. You couldn't keep 'em away.

- Not inviting everyone to a party, and this includes weddings. Every Wednesday we would check the local paper for wedding announcements, and every single one ended with "No local invitations are being sent; friends and family are invited to attend." You would also post the same thing in your local church bulletin. I read an advice col-umn that responded to the question, "How do I not invite my uncle's family?" The writer really wanted to know, "How do I keep from having kids at my wedding?" In the South, just give it up, 'cause Uncle Earle and his eighteen kids aren't missing a good party. They will be there with bells on and tell EVERYONE who listens, "I'm on the bride's side." If you are lucky, only his current wife will show up and not his three exes.

- Asking for an RSVP—I know you want a head count, but you aren't getting one! I'm from Mississippi, and we are very noncommittal about our comings and goings. We feel more comfortable saying, "We'll be there if the creek don't rise." Meaning, if nothing else comes up, then we'll be there.

  RSVP: Yes

  RSVP: No

  RSVP: If the creek don't rise

To counteract the lack of RSVPs, we have the most stunning buffet tables you've ever seen. I'm talking fruit-and-cheese displays that are three feet tall and ice bowls overflowing with peel-and-eat shrimp (it has to be peel-and-eat; otherwise, somebody is going to just stand there like it's the first time they ever saw shrimp). I remember the first time I laid eyes on the buffet at the Beau Rivage casino in Biloxi and thought, *Now, this is a buffet fit for a wedding*. It's not tacky to use store-bought food. Some of the South's best fried chicken can be found at a roadside gas station, and the best meat and three* is usually at the grocery store, but you still want to give it a nice presentation. If you don't have time to cook, that's fine, but it has to look good! Take the store-bought food and put it on a pretty platter, and for the love of all that is precious and holy, take the price tag off!

- Bringing food to a party when the hostess didn't ask you to. Everyone says, "What can I bring?" when being invited to a party. If the hostess says, "Just yourself," then you show up with your sweet self and a hostess gift.
- Asking a woman when she's having a baby, or when she's having another baby, or when she is due. Just smile and nod, and you will be made aware of baby news when it's time for you to know.
- Wearing white after Labor Day to church isn't technically tacky, but why would you want to have precious time wasted on having people debate your

---

* "Meat and three" is what you call a restaurant that serves your pick of meat and three vegetables at a fixed price. You also get a roll or cornbread and sweet tea.

clothes? Trust and believe that the conversation will be behind your back and you'll never know it, but it might open other transgressions. "Well, you know she did dance on those tables while she was at Auburn, and I heard she also wore black shoes on Easter Sunday," and all of this comes up because you wore white after Labor Day. Transition to winter white and let it be. The only exception is a whiteout football game, but this goes out to all of the athletic departments—telling ladies what to wear to a football game is tacky! We won't tell you that your team needs to run the ball, and you don't tell us what to wear.

- I learned the hard way that *not* owning a copy of *Southern Sideboards* is very tacky. The beloved cookbook was published by the Junior League of Jackson. Mississippi native Wyatt Cooper, who was an author and screenwriter before he was known for being Anderson Cooper's father, wrote the beautiful foreword that describes food and life in Mississippi.

When I first moved to Jackson, I worked at the Everyday Gourmet, which was co-owned by Ms. Dorothy

(Dero) and her daughter Carol. Ms. Dero Puckett was everything you ever pictured when you thought of a classic Southern lady. When the Jackson Symphony League was hosting Martha Stewart for their annual fundraiser, they needed someone to open their home, and everyone was scared to do so. Not Ms. Dero. She gladly opened her home and made a lifelong friend. I can remember after Hurricane Katrina, seeing Ms. Dero on Martha's television show talking about the devastation to her home in Pass Christian, Mississippi.

One day, we were looking at cookbooks, and I naively said, "Oh, I don't have this one," when looking at a copy of *Southern Sideboards*.

"I'm sorry—what did you say?" Ms. Dero exclaimed.

"I don't think I have this cookbook," I repeated, and she quietly whispered to me, "Don't ever let anyone hear you say that, and don't be caught with a brand-new copy of *Southern Sideboards*. Go run over it a few times with your car and make it look old, but never get caught with a new one."

I relayed the story to my mother. She was horrified. "Ellen! I have two copies of *Southern Sideboards* at my house. One is mine and the other is yours for when you are smart enough to know how to take care of it."

I relayed this back to Ms. Dero, and she was relieved. "I was surprised, as you seemed to have a very good raisin'. That is a good mama you have," she confided.

I'd love to tell you that this is a definitive list of all things tacky, but spotting tacky can be just as difficult as telling the difference between naggin' and mouthy. Truth be told, as soon as you think you've written the full list of all things tacky, someone will up and propose at their best friend's wedding.

18

KILL 'EM WITH KINDNESS

Hey, Jesus, it's me...I did it. I killed 'em with kindness. Just one question. Where do I hide the body?

We kill everyone with kindness in the South—
it's our calling card. A boy could say that the
sky is green, and we'd say, "And isn't it a lovely
shade of green!" Later, we would compare notes
with others and say something like "That boy
ain't right. He thinks the sky is green," and then
we'd discover that he has a rare eye disorder
that his mama never wanted anyone to know
about, but she did do an unspoken prayer
request for his eyes to heal, and everyone put
two and two together, so we just carry on and
act like he can see just fine.

RARELY WILL WE DISCUSS POLITICS, religion, or college football in polite company, because we want to keep the conversation nice and agreeable. I thought everyone did things this way until I met my mother-in-law, a Yankee from Upstate New York. The best part of having a Yankee mother-in-law is that you always know where you stand, and the worst part is that you always know where you stand.

Once I settled in, I found comfort in not needing to put on airs with her. I only knew her a few short years before she passed, but I made a promise to myself—that my kids would know her through the stories I remembered of her and the stories I'd heard from others.

When my kids' grandmother was due with their father on Christmas Eve 1973, and he still hadn't arrived on New Year's Eve, she told her husband, "Take me dancing!" She danced the night away and birthed the first baby born in Des Moines, Iowa, in 1974. Their grandmother was a pragmatic nurse who worked in the OR, so she wasn't easily distracted, and she was definitely not starstruck when a future Hall of Fame, allstar quarterback came in. The mouthy football player was met with a reality check because their grandmother knew kindness wouldn't work. She told him to cut the crap because he was acting like a donkey's butt, and he needed to straighten up. He said, "Yes, ma'am," and was the gentleman I'm sure his mama raised him to be.

When my kids are ready, I'll share her take on "girls' trips." "You do what you want when you get married," she told me, "but I never went on girls' trips." She went on to explain: "I remember I was so excited to go on one to the beach, but I was miserable the whole time." I asked why and she said, "All they did was complain about their husbands and their kids. It was like a contest to see who had it the worst at home. If you start looking for ways to complain about your husband," she told me, "then you'll find plenty."

Had she been Southern, the next time she was invited to go on the trip she would have made up an excuse, and the next time made up another excuse, then another, and eventually the ladies would have stopped asking and no one would have been any wiser. But she was not Southern, so when she was invited, she said, "Thank you so much for the invitation. I work long days at the hospital and cannot go on a girls' trip if all we're going to do is complain about our families." I'm sure there are husbands that would have been mortified by her candor, but not my father-in-law. He would smile and grin with each story. He may not have known exactly what he was getting into when he married her, but he had a good idea.

Most Southern women drop subtle hints to their boyfriends about hoping to get engaged and wondering when the big event will happen: "Oh, I'd love a spring wedding, but we'd have to start planning now." Or

"Mary Elizabeth just got engaged; maybe that will be me one day..." Not my mother-in-law. She got right to the point. After months of a long-distance relationship, she got off that plane and told her boyfriend, "If we're not engaged by the time I leave, I'm not coming back." Her Biloxi boyfriend loved her spunk. He put his arm around her shoulders and told her, "Well, let's go find you a ring."

She never met a bush worth beating around in her life. While other in-laws would say, "Let me share this recipe with you—you might like it," mine said, "Ellen, if Tim ever wants a chocolate cake, the best recipe is on the back of the Swans Down cake flour box." She was right. I substituted hot coffee for the warm water, and it is the best chocolate cake recipe on planet Earth. The chocolate buttercream on the box is spot-on as well. You might as well make every recipe on that box.

She also bought each of her three children a Fannie Farmer cookbook. Unlike my mother with a Smithsonian level of cookbooks, she only needed one, and it was the Fannie Farmer. She told me point-blank, "If there is something of mine that you want to cook, it probably came from there."

Each Christmas Eve, I pull out my Fannie Farmer

cookbook and turn to the coffee mallow recipe. While the marshmallows are melting, I tell my kids about their Yankee grandmother who never killed anyone with kindness but would bend over backward to help her friends and family.

Years after she passed, I heard a group of women going through the phone book with all their grievances against their mothers-in-law! "Let me tell you what mine said," followed by "Oh, that's nothing compared to mine!" They were each trying to top each other in the *My mother-in-law is worse than yours* championship.

Once those ladies came up for air long enough, they asked me, "You know what we mean, right? Is yours horrible too?" but I couldn't join in. I would give anything to have my Yankee mother-in-law back. It would mean that my husband still had his mom and that my kids would have two grandmothers. Even if I only had one more hour with her and right before the hour started, she called Tim to say, "Make sure Ellen eats because she gets really moody when she's hungry!"

It wasn't that easy when we first met, but we found our way. I was working at the Purple Parrot Cafe, which was the place to be in Hattiesburg. I can still see one of the doctors' wives gliding into the restaurant. She looked like the cat that ate the canary and couldn't wait to tell me that she ran into my new boyfriend's mother at the gym. "Oh, you've got your hands full with that one," she said. I asked what she meant, as Tim's mother had been nothing but nice to me in our few interactions.

"Well, I asked her if she was excited about Tim dating you because you know we just love you." *As they should. I kill every customer at the restaurant with kindness.* "And she told me that she didn't see how you two would ever work out." *What? That doesn't sound like the person I met.* "Yes, she told me that she didn't see you two working out."

Tim asked his mother what she meant by all that and she said, "I didn't mean anything by it except I don't see how you two will work because she works all the time. That doesn't mean I don't like her or don't want you to work out. It only means what I said."

"Well, Mom, when you stay stuff like that in the South, it sounds like you don't like her."

"Well, I'm sorry. I'm still from Upstate New York where 'I'm not sure how those two will work out' means 'I'm not sure how those two will work out.'"

Tim reported back to me his talk with his mother. He said, "Look, I'm sorry. My mother doesn't sugarcoat anything. I know it can be hard and it may seem like she doesn't like you, but she does. She just said the other day that she wished my brother could find someone like you."

But I was confused. "Your brother is married."

"I know," he said, "and Mom said—and I quote—'I wish your brother could find someone like Ellen.'"*

I never missed my mother-in-law more than the day I held my little boy, Nikolas (Nik) Skrmetti, for the first time. He was my second baby, and I was a more relaxed mother. I could enjoy this one. As soon as I put him in my arms, I felt him sink into me. I thought, *This must be how she felt when she held her little boy.*

I realized when I held him how generous she was when we first met. Holding my son, I understood how hard it must have been for my mother-in-law to let a new woman come into her son's life. I hope that when I have a daughter-in-law, I can be as straight to the point as she was. I pray I love her, but more importantly, I pray she loves me. And if we don't get along, I can always kill her with kindness.

---

* Tim's brother and his wife are now happily divorced and married to amazing people and still friends.

19
SOMMAY'ALL

Hey, Jesus, it's me. Listen, we were sitting in church the other day, and we were singing "When We All Get to Heaven." I know—I love it too. But it seems like some of the people in the church need to be singing "When Y'all Get to Heaven" or "When Sommay'all Get to Heaven," because I don't think everyone at my church is going to be in the sweet by-and-by...right? Am I going to see everyone on that heavenly shore?

W HEN THEY WALKED INTO MY
church, it took every ounce of grace
not to say, "If only you'd met Jesus
before her, then you might still be
married." Of course, I never said it. I wanted to, though.
I sat in the pew like a burnt biscuit thinking of the
things I would say if I got the chance. I also wondered
what they were doing at the First Baptist Church. I
had heard they were visiting churches, but I figured
they would go Methodist, Episcopalian, or Out of Town.

I know exactly why they picked our church. Typical.
Let one rogue Sunday school class get a reputation for
wife swappin' at small group, and every Tom, Dick, and
Mary wants to see if it's true. For the record, nothing
was ever confirmed. However, one of the couples is now
divorced, another moved out of town, and the Sunday
school teacher is now Episcopalian, so...confirmed.

Mark was my friend Marcy's ex-husband. She had caught him running around with another woman three years earlier, which resulted in their divorce. Now he had the gall to show up at my church with his new woman! In my eyes, she was just as guilty as he was. I don't care how much you pray—the Lord will never send you another woman's husband. Show me one passage in the Bible where God says, "I'm going to send you a man, but he's going to be on a trial separation. But really, he's practically divorced, because his marriage has been over for a long time, and it's better for his kids that he gets the divorce because it's not good for the kids to be raised in a home where the parents have fallen out of love. But what you aren't going to know is that by 'trial separation' he means that he's dipping his toes in the water to see if there is anything better on the market, and his wife thinks he's at work right now and she's at home thinking how lucky she is to have such a good husband who is willing to work late and go the extra mile for the family." Nope.

He may send you a divorcé but not until the ink is dry on the divorce papers and the healing has begun. What was this new wife thinking?

My husband leaned over and whispered, "Be nice."

I'm always nice, my eyes darted back at him. If looks could kill, he'd be on his back with both legs in the air.

As the service started, I prayed, *Dear Lord, let them just be visiting. Please let them hate this church and go somewhere else. This doesn't seem like the right church for them.* Maybe sometimes church, unlike *Cheers*, is where you go because *nobody* knows your name.

The congregation started singing "When We All Get to Heaven." I looked around and...they were singing it too. They seemed just as excited as I was about meeting Jesus. Surely to goodness I wouldn't have to see Mark's face in the hereafter.

My plan for after the service was to hightail it to the car and avoid both of them. *Lord, let me get through this service so next week I can get back to my regular church service with all of these people that I love!* The choir started "Just as I Am" and—*Oh, heavens to Betsy, what are they doing? Are they leaving? Going to the bathroom?*

Then I realized what was happening. *NOOOOOO-OOOOO!!!!!!!!!!! They are walking toward the front... Please be lost...talking to the preacher...Turn them away, turn them away—NOPE! They are praying. Oh no! It can't be...*

The music ended, and the preacher spoke: "Brothers

and sisters, I am so thankful to introduce to you Mark and Shelby Cross." *You wouldn't be thankful if you knew what I know.* "Mark has been looking for a home church for some time now, and I'm thankful that Mark and Shelby have welcomed me into their home for fellowship and to discuss joining our church. I'm excited to see what their future holds as members of our church. Shelby has asked to join based on the promise of a letter from her home church, and Mark has joined based upon a profession of faith and wishes to take part in believer's baptism. Can I get a motion to..."

Blah, blah. I wasn't listening anymore. *Can I get a motion to let me do the baptism?* I thought. *Let me dunk him in the water. I'll make it quick and painless.*

The ride home from church was dead silent. I spoke first: "I will not ask her to join the committee on committees. I will not. I'll be nice, but we're not decorating the church together or planning potlucks. She can run the shut-in sock drive and collect hard candy for seniors. The church may not be big enough for two mortal enemies, but we'll find a way to make it work."

"Are you listening to yourself?" my husband asked.

"Yes! He ruined my friend's life, and now I have to go to church with him and his jezebel!"

"He messed up big-time, but everyone deserves a church," Tim reminded me. "Aren't you the one that's always saying that WeightWatchers is like church because you are welcomed back no matter what you ate the day before?"

"Don't use my words against me. I also said that church is like going to the gym because you never want to go, but you're always glad you did! I'm not exactly a thought leader."

He did have a point, though. To this day, Weight-Watchers has never turned me away, no matter how many times I quit and rejoin. I've only heard of one person being asked to leave, and that was my friend Valerie. She was the only person to hop on the scale, gain weight, and protest. Most of us would hear "You've gained half a pound," and then we'd explain that it had been a rough week...there was a buffet...it was a Tuesday, but not Valerie. She would make them reset the scale and do it again.

She could not figure out how she was counting points and gaining weight. She went over her point tracker to show that she was tracking her food with precision. "See? Breakfast was this many points, I had a salad for lunch and got ten points back, so then I had a steak for dinner..."

"Wait." The staff member stopped her. "Did you give yourself back ten points for the salad? You still deduct points even if it's a salad."

"Are you crazy?" she said. "I'm not taking away points for eating a salad! I only ate it because I thought I was getting points back that I could use later in the day! Do you mean to tell me that you take away points for salads and vegetables?"

She left in a huff and has never returned. In all honesty, I'm sure they'd welcome her back. She's a Weight-Watchers legend.

My husband continued, "I know you, and I know that you want to support your friend, and you think that welcoming him into our church is going against her. You girls stick together tighter than the Mafia. But it's been three years since their divorce."

"And that makes it right? They get to break up a family, but it's been three years, so I have to act like nothing ever happened?"

"Well, yeah. It's church, not the country club. Everybody is welcome at church. Yes, it's been three years since the divorce, but Mark only met Shelby a year ago and just got married. She's not the reason for their divorce."

"How do you know all that?" I demanded.

"Mark is my friend. His running around caught me by surprise, but we're still friends. Look, I know you won't be happy until he's in front of the courthouse tied to a tree so you can throw tomatoes at him, but I promise you—he's had a rough few years, and he's just now getting back on his feet."

I felt horrible. I still hated Mark, but I felt horrible for thinking his new wife was a jezebel. I also felt bad that she had prayed for a husband and God sent her Mark. She is going to have a hard enough row to hoe with him by her side. She didn't need me shunning her at church. *Hey, Jesus, if I'm nice to her, can I please still hate him?*

That next Sunday, we ran into Mark and Shelby in the parking lot headed into church. I had talked to Marcy earlier in the week, and she shared that Shelby was great with their kids, and she liked her. She even told Mark that if he messed it up with Shelby, she'd marry him again and make him suffer a second public divorce.

If Marcy had found a way to get along with Mark, then I could too.

Service started with that familiar hymn: "When we all get to heaven, what a day of rejoicing that will be..." Instead of looking around to see who should be singing and who shouldn't be singing, I kept on worrying about my own self and hoped no one was wondering why my judgy self was singing the song.

20

UNSPOKEN PRAYER REQUEST

Hey, Jesus, it's me. Listen, you know when
people have unspoken prayer requests?
Would it help if we got more information
so that you'll know what they are praying
about? It would not? You know the need?
Well, ok. I just wanted to check...

W

ILLIAM FAULKNER ONCE SAID, "To understand the world, you must first understand a place like Mississippi." I would take that further and say, "To understand Mississippi, you must also understand a place like Ripley, Mississippi." There is no doubt in my mind that he was thinking about Ripley and Tippah County when he said this. While he was born in New Albany and called Oxford, Mississippi, home, his great-grandfather is buried behind the Ripley Pizza Hut, and the town of Falkner, Mississippi,* nestled inside Tippah County, was named after his great-grandfather.

Ripley in the '80s was a dream. We spent our summers

---

* There are conflicting stories about how the *u* was added to his name. One is that his first publisher added it by mistake, and he never corrected him and kept the *u* throughout his career. The second is that he added the *u* to sound more hifalutin. I personally believe it was a mistake that he never corrected. A Southern gentleman would never care so much about a *u* to add it to their name to sound better, but they would think so little of a *u* to not ask for a reprint of their work.

at the pool where it cost a dollar to get in and a sunburn to get out. Every birthday party in the spring and summer was held at the Tippah Lake pavilion. Birthday parties had drinks, cake, and if your mom was fancy, she bought a printed tablecloth from Walmart.

Everyone was at church every Sunday except for the Smith family. They owned the Green Old Field restaurant where every Baptist, Methodist, and Presbyterian met for Sunday lunch. Ripley was a one-service town, so the restaurant opened whenever the churches let out. By default, Baptists were always last to arrive, and by birthright, my mom made sure we were the last of the Baptists.

The Baptists are known for having the most long-winded pastors,* then you add in a music minister who likes to sing all five stanzas, and a few professions of faith, and we had no chance of getting to the restaurant early. And of course, we had my mama and her want/need to visit with every single member of the church. Many would think that "Go wait in the car" would mean *I'm almost done* but no. It meant *I'm tired*

---

* This is by sheer observation. Bless your heart if your pastor preaches longer than a Baptist preacher.

of watching you and your brother fidget and grab my skirt to leave, so go sit in the car and let me visit in peace. And if I can remember that I'm mad at you by the time I get to the car, then you are in big trouble, but chances are I won't remember, and I'll let your suffering in the station wagon be punishment enough.

Wednesdays were also a sacred day of the week. Every church had Wednesday services, so most businesses closed early on Wednesdays to give everyone time to get ready for Wednesday-night church. For us, the kids had Mission Friends, RAs or Royal Ambassadors for the boys, and GAs or Girls in Action, which graduated to Acteens. The adults had prayer meeting, which, to my dismay, was just that—prayer meeting. Mom let me go once, but before she agreed, she told me it wasn't fun and that I would be bored.

It took less than five minutes for me to realize that she was right. On the way into the sanctuary, they passed out a sheet of paper, and on it there were categories like Shut-In, Sick, In the Hospital, In the Nursing Home, with names under them. Then they had a deacon lead the prayer meeting who had NOT been skilled in the art of keeping a room's attention. He would say, "Let's pray for Ms. Edna, who is in the hospital."

I would whisper to Mama, "Why is she in the hospital? What happened?"

"SHHHH," she would whisper-yell. "We are praying!"

Then someone would say, "Be with Mr. Simpson in his time of need."

"What is his need?" I'd whisper again.

"Shut your eyes and bow your head."

"So I'm just supposed to sit here while they call out all these names? And they never say why they are on the list," I'd retort.

"We will discuss this at home."

Well, now my prayer was that prayer meeting would last long enough that she'd forget that we were going to discuss this at home. Was it too late to add that to the prayer list? *Pray for Ellen Goolsby, that her mama doesn't get on to her for being nosy at the prayer meeting, and she promises to not come back until she is mature enough to not ask follow-up questions.*

Lucky for me, all the prayer calmed her nerves, and she didn't mention my prayer-meeting questions. I still had to ask, "Mama, why *do* they just say the names at prayer meeting? Don't we need to give God more detail?"

"He doesn't need any of our detail. He is the detail.

Jesus knows every thought, every worry, every desire of our hearts. If you say, 'Lord, please be with my friend,' he'll know exactly *who* you are praying for, *what* you are praying for. All you have to say is, 'Hey, Jesus, it's me,' and he's going to know exactly who YOU are!"

"Ok, but what about the unspoken prayer requests—what about those?"

"Well, it's just an unspoken prayer request. Unspoken doesn't make it unknown. It's unspoken because there isn't a category for 'Please pray for my son who I'm sure you've all heard by now was supposed to graduate from college this semester, but he actually flunked out three semesters ago and has been living on campus high on the hog* and only came clean because we were coming into town for his graduation.' Or 'Please be with my daughter as she goes through rush at Ole Miss**— may it never rain, may her pantyhose never run, may a suntan line never show, and please, Lord, keep the pepper outta her teeth.'"

"And for the people that don't know *why* someone is on the unspoken prayer list?"

---

* This means he has been living a life of luxury. This saying started because the best cuts of meat are from the back of the hog.

** But seriously, pray for all ladies going through rush.

"It's ok because God knows their heart no matter if they were on the 'In the Hospital' or 'Out of the Hospital' list. Truly, you could say, 'Hey, Jesus, it's me. Listen, could you please be with my friend? I don't know why but I know you do, so please be with her,' and he will! He knows it's you, he knows the friend, and he knows the need."

"Ok—but why do you have to have a meeting? Why can't you just pass out the sheet of paper with people to pray for and say, 'Here, pray when you get home'?"

"It goes back to the Bible. Matthew 18:20: 'When two or more are gathered in my name, I'm there.' Yes, he hears our individual prayers, but we believe there is power in numbers, and when we gather for prayer meeting, we believe that God is going to help every person on the list! It's not a social hour—that's why I kept shushing you! We are praying together so that God hears our prayers, but also so that the people being prayed for FEEL the prayers."

It would be over twenty years before I understood what it meant to *feel* a prayer. I would hear people say, "Thank you for your prayers—we feel them," and I would smile and nod like I knew what they were talking about. I thought it was something you said, but I learned that you *can* feel prayers.

Nothing can prepare you for losing a loved one, but prayer can guide you. One morning I got a call from Mama. "Ellen," she said. The way she said my name, I knew this was going to be bad news. "Grandmaw Iris passed away last night. She didn't suffer, and we were with her the whole time." Grandma Iris was my mother's mother and one of the sweetest ladies I've ever known. She had seven grandchildren, and we all believed with all our hearts that we were her favorite. I was not prepared for the pain that I felt. As I was wilting, word was spreading through town that Ms. Iris had passed, and I could feel myself gaining strength as everyone in town began praying for our family. I went from being frozen with grief to being able to make plans to get home, pack my bags, and get to my family. Nothing on earth could prepare me to lose my grandmother, but prayer guided me.

I miss those days. Wednesday-night prayer meetings have gotten smaller, and the sanctity of Wednesdays has all but gone by the wayside. Banks and stores now would never dream of closing early on Wednesdays. For what? Church?? Why would they close early for church? There was a time we wouldn't have dreamed of playing a ball game on a Wednesday night, but now we'll play an entire tournament on Easter weekend.

Prayer meetings have turned to social media, where people like to ask for prayer for unspoken requests but also ask for privacy. I'm guilty of doing the opposite. I'll start looking at your husband's page, your sister's page, play Facebook detective to get to the root of the problem. I'll spend so much time playing detective that I forget to pray for the poor soul asking for prayer. We've replaced meaningful prayer with virtual hugs in the form of ((((((hugs)))))), and we've written *thoughts and prayers* so much that we've shortened it to *ts and ps*. Even better, in case praying for someone brings offense, we send hugs and vibes to people. I have felt my fair share of prayers, but I can't say that I have ever felt a ((((((hug)))))) or a vibe.

Social media is here to stay, but I hope we can always remember how much we need each other, how much we need to gather together in prayer and celebration.

Hey, Jesus, it's me. Listen, will you help us to never forget the power of talking to you?

Of giving you our worries and fears along with our hopes and dreams? Let us never stop praying for our friends and never stop gathering together for no reason other than to ask for your help.

Amen.

Conclusion
LET ME PUT ONE LAST BUG IN YOUR EAR

I SUBTITLED THIS BOOK *I HAVE QUES-tions, Comments, and Concerns* in the hope that you will take every question, comment, and concern straight to Jesus. By *every*, please know that I mean every! You cannot talk to Jesus too much. He will never get exhausted by you, he'll never let your prayer go to voicemail...but he may put your answer on hold. Stay faithful and he will answer.

Years ago, Tim had a good friend going through a tough time. I asked how he was doing, and Tim said, "Oh, he's fine. He's like you and he prays about everything."

Insert record scratch. "I'm sorry—what did you say?" *He did not just say what I think he just said.*

"Y'all were both raised Protestant and pray about every little thing." He went on to explain that he does pray about the big stuff, but he doesn't want to bother God with every little thing.

"Excuse me? Every little thing?" *Yes, he really did say what I thought he said.* "I'll have you know that it doesn't matter if you're Baptist, Catholic, or a heathen—God wants every little thing." I took a breath quick enough so that he couldn't get a word in and then reminded him that it was in a Catholic Mass at St. Richard's in Jackson, Mississippi, where Father Michael O'Brien told the entire parish, including Tim, that God wants every part of our life and that there is no prayer too small.

"Well, I just—" he said, trying to intervene, and God bless a man who tries to stop a Southern woman when she's on a roll. *Note to men—just let us get it all out of our system. It's easier on all involved.* My last and most important point to drive into my sweet husband's thick skull was to help him understand that I pray for him every night and every day, and he is supposed to be praying for our family every night and day, and the *only* reason I follow his lead is because I think he's praying, and he better get to praying for everything because that is how this works.

Ok, maybe I have been a naggin' wife.

Tim agreed to pray more, and I kept praying for him and our family. The change didn't happen overnight, but over time I could feel our situation shift. I wish I could tell you that we've had an easy road ever since, but there are plenty of times that I felt like I was only bringing concerns: *Hey, Jesus, it's me. Are you sure he heard you right? Could you please repeat it back, so I know that he heard the right thing?* On the rockiest of roads, we never felt Jesus leave our side.

I also hope that by giving Jesus all of your questions, comments, and concerns, you'll know his timing is always perfect, and it's never too late for Jesus to make a way. I used to wonder where I would be if I had never had stage fright and could have started this journey sooner. I quickly turn my thoughts to thankfulness for the now, because I wouldn't rewrite my life any other way.

So for you, dear reader, my prayer is that you know that whatever dream is on your heart, whatever goal you long to reach, as long as it isn't to win Miss Mississippi on your first try, all things are possible. You may see no way for your dreams to happen, but never forget that God will never leave you, and when you feel like giving up, you only need to bow your head, close your eyes, and say, "Hey, Jesus, it's me."

Acknowledgments

MY MOTHER, MARTHA GOOLSBY—thank you for getting behind every dream, even though it meant more work for you.

My father, Lonnie Goolsby—I don't know that anyone could work harder for their family than you did for ours. Thank you for the blood and sweat that you gave to give us everything.

My brother, Matthew—thank you for listening to every bad joke and walking this road with me. I have always felt bad that I would get clothes for Christmas while you got truck tires, guns, and speakers, and I appreciate you never being jealous about that.

Shannon Marven—you are truly my fairy book mother. Thank you for sliding into my DMs and becoming a mentor and friend.

Daisy, Patsy, and Jenny with Hachette Book Group—when I met you, I knew my stories would be in good hands.

Acknowledgments

Sydney Delahoussaye—thank you for all of your help and encouragement.

Bruce Ayers—thank you for making me a headliner.

Casey Shoemaker and Holland Goodrow—you are a marketing super duo.

Kristie Nutt and Carly Smith—thank you for being the best backup dancers/cheer section a girl could have.

Last but certainly not least, thank you to every single person that has followed me on social media. I appreciate each and every one of you and thank you for laughing with me.

About the Author

ELLEN SKRMETTI GOT HER START in comedy by making her customers laugh while working as an advertising representative for some of the best social magazines in Jackson, Mississippi, and Nashville, Tennessee. Once her family moved to Birmingham, she decided to get serious about comedy and studied stand-up comedy at the premier school of comedy, Second City. Her teachers and classmates helped her find confidence in telling stories of her colorful upbringing in the South. She had just started booking herself at comedy clubs when the 2020 COVID-19 shutdown happened. Although she thought her dream was over, she turned her comedy into social media sketches. After nine months of growth that was slower than molasses, her sketch "If the Queen Died in the South" went viral. She kept posting comedy and has never looked back. Still making millions laugh online, she also sells out live shows across the US.

She lives in Birmingham, Alabama, with her husband, Tim, and children, Meg and Nikolas.